LIKE FATHER, LIKE SON

Rediscovering Sonship
On The Fathering Journey

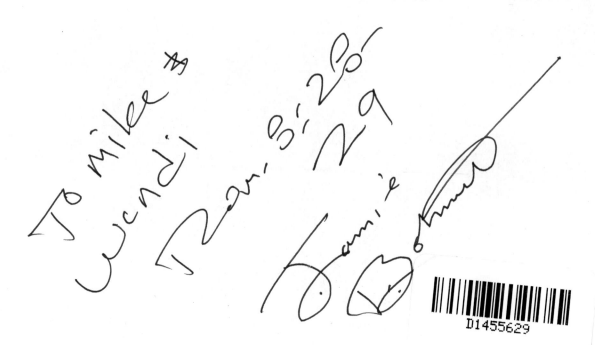

To mike &
Wendi

Rom 8:28-29

Jamie B.

LIKE FATHER, LIKE SON

Rediscovering Sonship
On The Fathering Journey

JAMIE BOHNETT
FOREWORD BY
KEN CANFIELD

Pleasant Word
A Division of WINEPRESS PUBLISHING

Pleasant Word (a division of WinePress Publishing, PO Box 428, Enumclaw, WA 98022) functions only as book publisher. As such, the ultimate design, content, editorial accuracy, and views expressed or implied in this work are those of the author.

Unless otherwise noted, all Scriptures are taken from the Holy Bible, New International Version, Copyright © 1973, 1978, 1984 by the International Bible Society. Used by permission of Zondervan Publishing House. The "NIV" and "New International Version" trademarks are registered in the United States Patent and Trademark Office by International Bible Society.

Scripture references marked KJV are taken from the King James Version of the Bible.

Scripture references marked NASB are taken from the New American Standard Bible, © 1960, 1963, 1968, 1971, 1972, 1973, 1975, 1977 by The Lockman Foundation. Used by permission.

ISBN 1-4141-0403-0
Library of Congress Catalog Card Number: 2005901203

DEDICATION

This book is dedicated to my Dad, F. Newell Bohnett. He is a man I have increasingly grown to appreciate and admire through the years. He is a decorated WW II and Korean War Marine Corps pilot, a co-founder of a national restaurant chain, and has been a Hawaii rancher and real estate developer, among other things. But I am just so proud to simply call him "My Dad."

TABLE OF CONTENTS

ACKNOWLEDGMENTS

A special thanks goes to Pete Pagan, who co-wrote with me the accompanying discussion guide and for his great help with the "polishing up" of this book.

Thank you to my "Successful Living™ coach, Michael Van Skaik, for "cracking the whip" to get this done.

Thank you to the dads who were willing for their stories to be used for this book and the small group discussion guide, to Dan, Marvin and Jeanett, David, Chris, Duane, Rick, Steve, Brad, Pete, Michael, Ken, and Gary.

Thank you to Mike McConnell, who was the first to fervently pray for me and prod me to write this book.

Thank you to my special email prayer partners who have held me up in prayer during this time, to Brad, Cale, Don D. Don W., David, Jeff, John, Ken, Pete, Kay, my sister Lynda, Nola, Paul, Rick, Sarah, Sky, Heidi, Steve, Sue, and Tom.

Thank you to the men of Northshore Baptist Church who were willing to let me test out this "Like Father, Like Son" material on them each week like "Guinea Pigs"—I love you guys!

Thank you to my manuscript readers, Paul Eklund, Ken Knuckey, Pete Pagan, and Michael Van Skaik, and my dear pastor, Jan Hettinga who were all willing to read this manuscript, investing their valuable time to provide invaluable feedback.

Thank you to the trustees of the Bohnett Memorial Foundation, F. Newell Bohnett, Owen Johnston, Tom Bohnett, Joe Bohnett and Bill Bohnett for all of your great encouragement and support.

A special thanks goes to my dear friend, Dr. Ken Canfield, founder and president of the National Center For Fathering. Thank you for your willingness to write the foreword for us and for the many "seeds" you have planted in my life and ministry, through your faithful and courageous pioneering work that you have done in the fathering field

A big thanks go to awesome kids, Heidi and Sky, Adam, Jeremy and Holly, who have each in their own ways encouraged me to write this book and, with all of my shortcomings, to accept me as I am…and that inspires me to do better than I have done.

I need to thank two very special people who now live in heaven—my" Grandma Vi," Violet Bohnett, who encouraged me and believed in me when I didn't believe in myself. You forever blessed me with the power of your loving words. And my dear mother, Nada Bohnett. I miss you deeply, Mom. Your persevering prayers and patient love brought me to know your Lord more than I ever was able express to you in your earthly life. The Violet R. & Nada V. Bohnett Memorial Foundation is named after these two special women, and I am proud to keep their earthly legacy alive through the work of the Foundation.

Last, but not least, I thank my awesome, beautiful wife and best friend, Cindy, for all of your loving support and prayers and for saying "Yes" to me thirty plus years ago and saying "Yes" again to us eight years later when it all appeared hopeless. Cindy, it is truer than ever, "We've only just begun!"

FOREWORD

Most committed dads go about their business quietly and faithfully. Some people notice that they're great dads, but too often we don't give them the honor they deserve until something tragic happens.

You may remember the family that was driving one rainy night on a Kansas interstate highway when their van was swept off the road in a flash flood. When the father, Robert Rogers, kicked out his window so he could help everyone escape, he was sucked out of the van and away from his family. His wife and four children were trapped inside, and they all perished.

Now, think for a moment, Dad, how you would react and keep on living if something like that happened to you.

I met Robert not long ago, and he's a hero. Sure, he has had many tearful, lonely nights, but he has said repeatedly that he has no regrets. He can look at his life before the accident and honestly say, "I was the best dad I could be for eight years." Here's a dad who has truly lived with no regrets! And that's where the hero part comes in.

How did he do it? He says, "We savored every moment as a family. We prayed together and memorized Bible verses together nightly as we snuggled before bedtime. We went camping, fishing, and boating often. We lived life passionately, capturing every available minute with our kids. As an engineer, I'd travel some, but I didn't live to work. I worked to live."

This Job-like situation has taught Robert to trust God with everything. As he says, "My decision has been to live with gratitude. I have so much to be thankful for."

Now I know many of us get caught up in daily routines and sometimes miss our kids. We look toward some day in the future when we anticipate making more money or being less busy and we say, "Maybe then I can catch up with my kids. That's when I'll really work on being a better dad."

Obviously, this story shows us that tomorrows don't always come and we can't let important things wait. We have to live with no regrets, and I believe this book can help us do that. Jamie Bohnett addresses foundational, essential truths here, such as the importance of your relationship with your father. Understanding that relationship — or, at least, coming to terms with the shortcomings of that relationship – is where all successful fathering journeys should begin.

Then, as Jamie urges us, we must be painstaking about making sure we're providing our children with the love, guidance, and support that they need. Too many of us fathers are on cruise control. We don't make our children a top priority or make the most of every opportunity we have with them.

The reality check does come for all of us. For some, it's in the later years when the children are all grown and they are reflecting back on their lives, evaluating what they have accomplished and what they would do differently. That's when so many men say that they would trade all their possessions and accomplishments in the business world for a chance to go back and bond with their children. They can repair things, in a sense, but they can never go back.

If we're lucky, the reality check will come sooner as happened not long ago for a United States Congressman I know. After an event at which I was speaking about the importance of fathers, he told me how he has not been the father he wants to be. We can imagine how a dad in his position might struggle to make time for his children in the midst of all the different people pulling at him for his best time and energy. But it's really what we all face in one way or another.

Well, this congressman's wife told him about two events that happened when he was away, and it pierced his heart. One of the events was a picture drawn by his five-year-old son, a picture of their family – except there was no dad. When his mother asked, "Where's Dad?" the boy replied, "He's in Washington."

Then, a few days later — while the congressman was caught in an extended session of debates and meetings — his wife told their son, "Dad should be home soon." But the boy replied, "Dad's not coming home. He's in heaven."

All this congressman could do was shake his head, because while he did want to make a difference for the people in his district, many of his daily obligations suddenly didn't seem nearly as important as being there to father his children.

That was his wake-up call. I know another father who came home one day and didn't recognize his own son playing across the way in the back yard. Or, there's the football coach who came home late and went in to see his son sleeping in bed. He was shocked at how tall his son had grown and was almost moved to tears when he thought about all he was missing out on.

Dad, I believe these moments of realization that help us rearrange our priorities are right from the heart of God. And if you've never gotten a wake up call like that, I recommend that you keep reading! I believe this book will give you a startling reality check that brings all your priorities into focus.

Jamie Bohnett has been a good friend and a fathering advocate since the early years of the National Center For Fathering. I know his wife and family. He is a father with integrity. He has also been a strong leader of men in the Northwest and has helped us refine our small-group materials as he tests them with real dads on a week-by-week basis. Most of all, he grasps the truth that God has a heart for fathers, and He has destined that we multiply ourselves — not just physically, but spiritually.

I want to encourage you as you read ahead. A study from the University of Virginia concluded that faithful, churchgoing fathers are exceptional fathers. I suppose we shouldn't be too surprised; after all, the Bible urges us to place our families as a high priority. The church is a natural pro-family support network. And, as this researcher said, religion helps domesticate men and makes us more receptive to the needs and aspirations of our wives and children.

So what do we do with this research? We can thank God for softening our hearts and giving us His Spirit to lead us as we seek to be the fathers our children need. And since there are no perfect fathers here on earth, we should continue to make fathering a priority. That means being more aware of our children's unique qualities, more attentive listeners, and more active in helping them develop their spiritual disciplines and love for Jesus. We can renew our commitment to pray for them daily.

As fathers of faith we may have some advantages, but we cannot rest on our laurels. For each of us there is always room to grow. Training our children to serve Jesus with their lives is a high calling. This book will make a big difference as we seek to do that.

—Ken R. Canfield, PhD.
President
National Center For Fathering
Fathers.com

INTRODUCTION

We live in the most "unfathered" generation of American history—not because of natural disaster or through war or disease but by the selfish choices that men have made without concern of how those choices would affect their children. So many fatherless or "fatheredless" men are now fathers themselves without a clear picture of what positive father involvement looks like. I believe, because of this reality, "job one" for men today is to reorient their lives to Another Father, the heavenly Father, who is the "True North" of fatherhood. He is the only true corrective for a man's distorted personal experiences and perverted cultural images of what a father's role is to be in the lives of his children.

Through the pain that grown sons feel today, I have come to firmly believe that men, especially those who are now fathers themselves, are being called and drawn to Another Father, the heavenly Father, through His Son, Jesus Christ. I have observed that a man's role as a son of his natural father, and his grappling with his own fatherhood, can become powerful tools in the heavenly Father's hands to awaken a man to discover his need for Another Father.

There are three basic things I want to address in this book.

First, I desire that fathers be able to explore the likeness that they have to their own biological fathers, to build upon the positives received from them and to turn from the negatives. I believe that before a man understands this clearly he is unable to know the extent of the heritage that he can access through his biological lineage. Also, unless a man examines his fathering heritage, he will not have a clear grasp of where the biggest struggles with sin in his life most likely will lie. A man's "default position" is set in a sinful tendency inherited from his father, grandfather, and great-grandfather, and ultimately back to Adam himself. It takes conscious choices of purposeful repentance to make a lasting life transformation.

Second, I want to show fathers the incredible power that they possess to impact their children. For every father it is no longer "just about me." We need to realize that there are huge implications upon the next generation from every decision we make-and that realization is a good thing.

Third, I want us as fathers to choose to embrace another fathering heritage made available through Jesus Christ, the Son of God. By so doing, we will become like Another Father. It is a liberating truth that no matter what our original fathering heritage might have held, or what our current culture tells us, we can be transformed to become like the heavenly Father when we submit ourselves to His Son, Jesus, and live out a lifestyle of repentance and obedience. We can become modern day "Joshuas" turning from the path of our fathers and the destructive path of our surrounding culture and proclaim, "…choose for yourselves this day whom you will serve, whether the gods your forefathers served beyond the River, or the gods of the Amorites, in whose land you are living. But as for me and my household, we will serve the LORD" (Joshua 24:15b NIV).

If you were a puzzle piece, how would you be able to figure out your life purpose? You would certainly not look within yourself. That would tell you nothing. There would be two basic ways you could figure out who you really were. First, you would look up and see on the box the big picture of what the puzzle is to look like, what the artist has in mind. Second, you would look around, above and below you to see how you fit with the other pieces of the puzzle. That is what I am challenging men to do in *Like Father, Like Son*. We will be looking to "the picture on the box," the heavenly Father as revealed through His Son in the Bible, to gain his grand perspective on who He is and what He desires to do in our lives as fathers. But also, we will be looking around us, to that puzzle piece right above us, to our father and how we are like him. Then we will look to those pieces below us, our children, and consider how we influence them to be like us.

Now a little bit about those male puzzle pieces above me. My Grandpa Floyd, on my father's side, was an entrepreneur who had his own heavy construction business in northern California. He had four sons and, when his sons were nearly adults, rather than continue to be away from the family, he chose to sell his business and move to Santa Barbara and develop a family business involving his sons. He later served on the city council there and became the mayor of Santa Barbara. My memories of Grandpa are positive. He was not very expressive to us emotionally but he was a hard working, talented man who deeply cared about the welfare of his family. For the most part he left the "touchy feely" stuff to my Grandma Vi. However, I can recall leaning against his stomach as he watched television on his recliner and he would rub my head until I couldn't feel it anymore!

On my mother's side, my namesake, my Grandpa Jim, was an immigrant from Yugoslavia. He also was an extremely hardworking man who built a successful restaurant business. I felt more loved by him than by my other grandpa, but he could also be a bit insensitive at times. He was a gruff, self-made immigrant who made good. He was a proud man who could make you laugh and cry. Like my Grandpa Floyd, he was a man who was deeply committed to his family. It was only years later that I realized that whenever he grabbed my cheek and shook it that this was a Yugoslavian way of showing affection. As a child I just thought it a bit weird.

My father, like his father, was a very hardworking entrepreneur who co-founded a restaurant chain that one day would be national in scope (Sambo's Restaurants, Inc.). He was also a decorated Marine Corps pilot in WWII and in the Korean War. That gave him an extra edge of "shape up or ship out" in his parenting style and an anger that could be awfully intimidating when it was aroused, which fortunately for us was not that often. He said military-like things to us kids all the time, like "saddle up troops" (translation: "Let's all get in the car") and "Who's gotta go to the head?" (translation: "Who needs to use the bathroom before we leave?"). He was highly motivated to succeed in his career, and succeed he did. He saw his role as a father primarily as a provider and left most of the nurturing and the day-to-day discipline to my mother. He had seen the providing role modeled very well by his father and he followed in his father's steps by working hard to provide for the needs of his family.

My Own Fathering Journey

My wife and I met in a church youth group. I was 19 and my wife was 17 when we married. We then went to a Bible college and I worked for my father in the family restaurant business. In retrospect, I realize that a major part of my wife's motivation for getting married was to escape some of the issues going on in her home and not so much to marry such a wonderful guy as myself!

When we had been married for about eight years and had a four-year-old daughter, Heidi, my wife, Cindy, was then in her mid-20's with a little girl to take care of all the time. Many of the issues she had suppressed started coming out, and she expressed to me that she did not want to be married any longer. As she slipped into depression, she did not even desire the identity of being a mother. By then my attitude had become complacent, cynical, and I was very critical of my wife.

This was a time when it would have seemed to make sense for us "to cut our losses." We really did not feel any love for each other any longer. We now admitted that we had probably married too young. We had changed into two completely different people in the past eight years. However, there was just one problem for me as I considered my options. It was that little four-year-old girl named Heidi sleeping innocently in her room. One night I walked into her room to look at her as she lay there and I sensed a strong impression, that I believe came from

God Himself, that if we moved ahead with divorce our daughter would be the innocent one who would suffer.

It just so happened by "coincidence," (even though I don't believe in coincidences, but rather in "God-incidences") that our pastor was starting a class for fathers. If he had said, "We are going to have a marriage class," I wouldn't have gone because Cindy wouldn't be there. And I just knew that *she* was our main problem. If only *she* would change, then our marriage could be healed, I foolishly thought.

But God was about to do something with me! As I began to meet each week with these men and my pastor, I realized a couple of things that changed my life. I saw that I needed to "get the log out of my own eye" when it came to my marriage. I had enough to work on without worrying about my wife, Cindy, and what *she* needed to work on. I also saw that in order for me to be a better father I needed to be a better husband. I was tricked; it was a marriage class disguised as a fathering class!

The power of the prayers of others for me, the word of God, honest confession, and repentance began to work. I was changed so much that Cindy began to notice and she began to get a glimmer of hope for us. Because I began to work on my issues, she now felt "safe" to work on her challenges without my critical attitude constantly oppressing her. It took a long time for feelings of love to return, but it was a start.

I stopped blaming my wife and started taking responsibility for the state of our marriage and family. She could have hardened her heart, but thankfully she did not. Deciding to be a faithful father, to turn my heart to my daughter at a critical time in our marriage, changed my whole life and family destiny! Even if my wife's heart had not turned back to me, I had changed, and that is why I am so passionate today about the need for all fathers to grasp the opportunity for personal life transformation that marriage and fatherhood make uniquely possible.

Cindy and I recently celebrated our thirtieth wedding anniversary. We have four children and now have a grandchild (Ellie Lani, the world's cutest grandchild). That little four-year-old is now married to a godly young man and is a new mother herself. Not only am I a changed person from this humbling experience, but the destiny of an entire family was transformed—four children grew up in the security of a loving (though not perfect) home and a Christ-following heritage has begun to be passed on to another generation. Every one of our four children is a unique and special individual. Each has been the heavenly Father's gift to my life. I am reminded continually by the Father that I have been given to them and that I have an irreplaceable, though constantly changing, role to play in their lives.

My wife and I have dedicated our lives to helping other couples to have vision for their marriages and families. We know that it was the Lord who rescued and redeemed our family from the pit of our pride and foolish rebellion. In gratitude for His mercy we feel most fulfilled when we share with others the same hope we found in our time of need.

SECTION 1

BUILDING THE HUSBAND-WIFE PARENTING TEAM— FIRST THINGS FIRST!

Putting "first things first" for a father is to build a strong marriage. From the very beginning of fatherhood there will be the temptation to pull away from the marriage relationship. The tendency is for the man to be drawn back into his work and for the wife to form a stronger bond with her children than she has with her husband. This is dangerous. Many fathers have lost access to their children because they have not tended to their marriage relationship and have not made their wives needs a priority. Many learn this too late. Yet there are some who wake up just in time. Dan is such a man. Listen to his story in his own words.

"The defining moment for me in my marriage was the first time I began to pull away from my parents' control of my life. This happened shortly after I became a parent for the first time. My daughter was about six months old and we had been married about a year and a half. I took a real stand, and tried to make a complete turn around. But I was so used to living that other way (the way I had learned from my family of origin).

My wife opened my eyes. She encouraged me and challenged me to stand up to my parents regarding how we were going to raise our daughter and lead our married life. That didn't go over too well at first. I sided with my parents for quite a while, until it was "them" or "us." I finally decided to go with "us," our family, my wife, my daughter and me. When I made that decision I realized that I could no longer play both sides.

But there wasn't an immediate change. I would go back and forth. Before we got married, I portrayed to my wife what I wanted to be rather than what I really was. The truth came out after we got married. My dad had often said, "Don't you ever turn your back on us." And now in my mind I had. He had based everything on conditional love. He was talking about inheritance and I couldn't care less about that.

After several months my wife saw that I was getting stronger, but I still had doubts. My mom kept planting concerns in me, but I was fighting it. I started to meet with a fathering group that helped me realize that while growing up I really did not have a healthy father figure in my life. The direction I got from the materials and the small group meetings also helped me to deal with the bigger issues and gave me hope.

Then we went to marriage counseling. For me the core issues were selfishness and laziness. I needed to change and our marriage had to change. I fought the changes all the way. The real help came when I met a man who began to mentor me in loving my wife and taught me the importance of the biblical principle of "leaving and cleaving." I keep a picture that friend took of my wife and me when we were in one of his parenting classes. That picture reminds me of our commitment to one another. I really focus on that when any of the old issues come up.

I see now that my father played the role of enabler in my life. If we were at some family function and an argument came up, he would always agree with me against my wife. It soon would get the better of him and he would decide to just leave. It doesn't take much to guess what my default mode of operation was for handling conflict in my marriage. I fell into being just like him. If yelling didn't work, then I withdrew. I almost lost my marriage doing that."

Dan almost lost the priceless treasure of his marriage, and if he had, no matter how much he may have wanted to be a good father, he would have become severely handicapped in his role. Building a strong marriage partnership is truly putting "first things first."

Thankfully, Dan's wife graciously allowed him room to grow when their marriage was in a fragile state. Dan has made a shift from following the pattern of his earthly father by default to now following the ways of the heavenly Father through faith in His Son. "Like father, like son" was true of Dan before, but now it is also true as he becomes increasingly like Another Father, his heavenly Father.

A note to single, non-custodial fathers: An unmarried father should not interpret this upcoming chapter as a discouraging, "guilt-inducing" message. It is very challenging to be a committed father without living with his children's mother but not impossible. A single father's commitment is more important than ever now to the life of his child. As a single father relies upon God's strength, he can make it a point to honor his child's mother and to have a civil relationship and parental partnership with her. "If it is possible, as far as it depends upon you, live at peace with everyone" (Romans 12:18 NIV).

Chapter 1

LOVING UNCONDITIONALLY

"Husbands, love your wives, just as Christ loved the church and gave himself up for her"
(Ephesians 5:25 NIV).

What Is Spiritually at Stake in a Marriage?

One question that has not been asked enough in our culture of divorce is how the splitting up of mom and dad affects a child's view of the Triune God. Does a father who leaves his wife and remarries another woman put a stumbling block in the path of a child's faith in the heavenly Father? What about a father who never commits to his child's mother in the first place, moving in and out of his child's life like a shadowy ghost? What kind of view of God is that child left with?

Imagine the child who grows up in a home where Mom and Dad stay together but the marriage is characterized by control and abuse. The child will tend to transfer his or her feelings of fear and resentment from his earthly to his heavenly Father. If that father has treated his wife with withdrawal and neglect, the mother will typically turn to her children, not out of strength but out of weakness, and will often become a "smother mother." No doubt children receive distorted views of God when this occurs.

The God of the Bible is revealed as an eternal, triune relationship of Father, Son and Spirit. The way God chose to reveal His image was through the creation of male and female living in a one-flesh relationship of husband and wife (Genesis 1:28-29). When this picture is shattered, then there is a direct hit on a child's view of God, hindering the formation of his godly character (Malachi 2:15-16).

What is at stake for the child in the mom-dad relationship is his balanced view of God's masculine and feminine attributes. A shattered husband-wife relationship leaves a child with a broken, cracked view of God.

The Tragedy of Divorce for the Children

Two years after divorce, seventy percent of fathers disconnect from their children; five years later ninety percent become disconnected. The children of divorce cry out in pain, pleading for fathers not to forget them. They want parents to work on protecting their marriages.

Listen to the cry of a sixth-grade writer in one of the National Center For Fathering's essay contests:

Everybody in my family has had to put up with all the things that have gone wrong. One thing about this divorce is that when I go over to my friend's house to spend the night or something, their fathers usually come in and say "good-night," not "good-bye." When my father comes over to get something and he is about to leave, he always comes over and kisses me on the cheek and then says "good-bye" and walks out. It hurts a lot. Sometimes I want to just cry. I wish this had never happened.

Contrast that pain with the sense of security reflected in an essay written by another of the Seattle essay contest's winners, a ninth-grade girl.

"I am safe. I am secure. I am loved. I am all these things because of my dad." She continues, "My dad is a very loving person. My mom and dad have been married for nineteen years, and I am sure that thirty-one years from now they will be celebrating their fiftieth wedding anniversary, loving each other just the same."

There is no doubt that today marriage is under attack from every side, and much has been written over the past three decades to try to come to its rescue. Many of these books have been written to men and women together, but the sad fact is that only women read the large major-ity of the marriage books. These books have not addressed the specific challenge facing MEN in marriage. They have not dealt with the motivational challenges facing a man to love one woman for a lifetime.

For generations the social stigma against divorce kept marriages together. The decision in 1973 to allow no-fault divorces changed all of that. Today, divorce and cohabitation are very common and carry no significant social consequences. Celebrities lead the way in what has come to be called "serial marriage," in which a man or woman has several spouses over a lifetime—not all at any one time, but for different periods of their lives. In northern Europe, seen as more "progressive" and "liberated," couples choose cohabitation more often than marriage.

My wife and I were deeply touched by the film, "The Notebook." The moving thing about the film to me was that Noah, the husband played by James Garner, loved his wife sacrificially through the disease of dementia to the very end. There was clearly very little in the relationship left "for him" except the pain of being a stranger to the one woman he had loved his entire adult life.

The problem with most marriage books is that the primary appeal is *self-fulfillment*. They make the assumption that a lifetime marriage is the primary path to real self-fulfillment. So the emphasis in these books is on things like conflict resolution, good communication, sexual techniques, and understanding basic male-female differences. While all these are very important, they do not touch a man's deepest motivation. They cannot make a man into a "Noah."

Marriage Motivation for Men That Will Last a Lifetime

Marriage is the heavenly Father's gift to allow a man to come into an increasingly deeper understanding of the Son's love for him. The challenge to learn to love one woman sacrificially for a lifetime will cause what a man intellectually knows about God's sacrificial love for him to be absorbed into the depths of his very mind and heart. Also, as a man grows in his insight into Christ's love for him and his wife, it enables him to love his wife freely from the heart. The two work together.

It is interesting that if we take the English word "married" in English and, symbolizing divorce, we remove the letter "i," we are left with the word "marred." Divorce has deeply wounded men, women, and families in America, especially during the past forty years. But even more significantly, divorce has marred a beautiful picture of the triune God, One Person, in intimate community of Father, Son, and Holy Spirit.

The quest for self-fulfillment cannot fuel a sustained and growing motivation for a man to love his wife for a lifetime. Jesus made it clear that intimacy with Him is not found through seeking self-fulfillment but by being willing to self-sacrifice. "If anyone would come after me, he must deny himself and take up his cross daily and follow me" (Luke 9:23 NIV). Marriage is designed by the heavenly Father to daily bring a man to face his self-centeredness and give him the opportunity to rely upon the resurrected life of Christ to transform him. The only way that a man can be motivated to love his wife for a lifetime is for him to keep his focus upon the goal of pleasing the heavenly Father and not himself.

A Covenant, Not a Contract

Marriage in our culture is viewed as merely a contract between two parties. The arrangement is viewed as conditional, with many escape clauses for one or both of the parties if they no longer are satisfied with the arrangement. This is not Covenant Marriage. A Covenant Marriage is built upon a promise that involves not just two, but three parties: a husband, a wife, and God. It is a relationship that reflects the mystery of Christ choosing His Church to be His bride. A

Covenant Marriage can be broken only by the death of one or both of the partners. It is a sacred commitment between a man and a woman and God. Marriage, to reflect God's highest design, needs to be seen as a covenant, a special three-way partnership. But beyond this there needs to be a special "covenant ethic" for the husband and wife to draw upon as they live together. In Hebrew the word that defines that ethic is "hesed" - or "loyal love" or "loving loyalty." In English the word is almost untranslatable, although the term "loving kindness" comes close. It is an undying love that fulfills its duty while at the same time it is a loyalty inflamed with love.

> Listen to what Paul Stevens says in his helpful book, *Married For Good*,
> "Hesed means living up to covenant obligations. It is not just affection, but affection plus faithfulness; not just sentiment, but sentiment plus service. Hesed goes beyond feelings to embrace commitment. Hesed is the mortar that holds the stones of the covenant in place.

> And Stevens continues,
> Without Hesed, few couples would survive the "for worse" experiences. The lean periods of a marriage…are the indispensable prelude to renewal and a deeper relationship. The irrevocable covenant is not a padlock but a safety net."[1]

Today we have marriages that are contracts but not covenants. We also have couples seeking to live out covenant without practicing Hesed. We live in a world where people are enslaved to selfish individualism. We are obsessed with our rights and are concerned largely with "looking out for number one." Once the emotional high, physical attraction and infatuation between a man and a woman wear off, most couples have little to build upon. The husband who has been drawing his strength to love from the love that his wife gives him soon finds that the well becomes dry. Covenant without Hesed can be a type of a relational prison where both parties can destroy one another with no way out. That, of course, is not an answer.

So the following is what it looks like for a man to live out Hesed in covenant using the timeless truths of the Ten Commandments as his guide.

The Ten Commandments for "A Husband of Hesed"

1. Thou Shalt Love thy Wife in Response To God's Love For Thee

> "I am the Lord your God, who brought you out of Egypt, out of the land of slavery. You shall have no other gods before me"
>
> (Exodus 20:2 NIV).

This first commandment is more than just a "preamble." It is the very foundation of all of the triune God's commands. A holy God has chosen to love a sinful people. It is an invitation to intimacy that cost God's Son His very life. Jesus, the Second Person of the triune God, gave

His life on the cross, experiencing the punishment for sin that every human being deserved. Just as the Israelites were held captive in Egypt, sin holds us all in its oppressive slavery. Our lives are literally a living death (death is separation from God) until the heavenly Father mercifully delivers us. The commandment points back to Israel's deliverance and also points ahead to the believer's deliverance through Christ.

To be able to love his wife faithfully for a lifetime, a Husband of Hesed must drink deeply and continuously from the wellspring of the love that God, who has chosen to die for him, has for him. "This is love: not that we loved God but that he loved us and sent his Son as an atoning sacrifice for our sins…and we know and rely on the love God has for us" (I John 4:10,16 NIV).

Knowing the fate he truly deserves, every husband needs to experience the quiet, grateful awe and wonder of being loved sacrificially by the God of the universe. The first commandment reminds a husband that he has been called to an undeserved relationship with God the Father through His Son. This is to be the source of love for his wife, not his wife's worthiness to be loved. The husband is to respond to that constant Father love and not simply respond to his wife's sporadic human love. He is to be so secure in being loved by God that he will be able to love his wife out of this strength rather than demanding to be loved by her.

I remember the first time my own weak love for my wife hit the wall. It was just after the birth of our first child. We were separated from family and friends, and she underwent an unexpected, severe postpartum depression. She changed completely from the happy, outgoing person she had been to someone I hardly recognized. We did not know how long she would be feeling this way or if this was going to be the "new normal" for Cindy. I can remember my mind racing with thoughts like, "I didn't sign up for this. She is a totally different person than the woman I married just three years ago!" But one day as we were taking a long drive with our new baby, both of us trying to make sense of what she was going through, a well-known song, "Just The Way You Are," by Billy Joel, popped up on the radio. It was if it was the heavenly Father Himself speaking to me through the lyrics of this soft rock song. It spoke powerfully to me of unconditional love in a relationship and I realized that is the love God had for me and that was the love I was to extend to my wife.

Through that song, I heard God's loving concern for me and His call for me to love my wife with that same love. Up to that point in our marriage I think I let Cindy's love fuel our relationship causing me to become lazy and passive. She, not the heavenly Father, had in effect become my "god" from whom I drew my love and strength to love.

The relationship with my wife needs to be the highest priority, but I cannot look at it as my source. I will need to learn not to *demand* her affirmation, love, and respect. I need to continually ask myself, "am I loving her in response to the heavenly Father's love for me, or am I depending upon her to love me first so I can simply respond?"

That is a tough question but it goes to the core of the issue. To check up, I continually ask myself, "Who is my God, my 'first cause'? Is it my wife or my heavenly Father?"

2. Thou Shalt Accept Thy Wife as She Is (Not for What Thou Desirest Her to Be)

"You shall not make yourself an idol"

(Exodus 2:4 NIV).

Although this also relates to the first commandment, this second commandment takes a slightly different slant as it relates to a husband's tendency to focus upon what he sees rather than upon the unseen.

This is one way that a husband struggles with idolatry. After he meets his wife and falls in love with her as a beautiful young woman, he is eventually faced with the inevitable. Both his wife's outward beauty and his own striking good looks eventually begin to fade. A wife's sexual desire naturally ebbs and flows, as does a husband's—even with all of today's modern medical helps.

The temptation for a husband is to not "see" the true person that he is married to within that aging body and to not focus on the true source of lasting beauty, his wife's spirit. Many men today are hopelessly in bondage to an image of youth and beauty while they allow their love for their wife to fade. A husband can become enslaved by admiring and desiring younger women who fit this mental image. He can soon find himself resenting and rejecting his wife because she can never possibly match the image that he worships.

A Husband of Hesed consciously recognizes that in a world that idolizes youth and beauty, he is the one man whom God has placed in his wife's life who daily is privileged to remind her of her true, unfading beauty and her infinite worth in the eyes of the heavenly Father and of himself. (I Peter 3:3-4)

I recall our wedding day, August 3, 1974. Our pastor told us that the rings on our fingers represented our married lives. The outside of the ring would be scratched and dented but the inside would become increasingly smooth. He forgot to tell me that over time my finger would become so fat that I would never be able to take the ring off! But the real me, the real Cindy, the real us as a couple, is like the smooth parts on the inside of the rings which have become more shiny and attractive in God's sight. "Therefore we do not lose heart. Though outwardly we are wasting away, yet inwardly we are being renewed day by day…So we fix our eyes not on what is seen, but on what is unseen. For what is seen is temporary, but what is unseen is eternal" (2 Corinthians 4:16,18 NIV).

I can honestly say that my wife is more beautiful to me today as the "whole package"—body, soul, and spirit, than on that day back in August of 1974. As she grows in internal beauty she continues to become more beautiful to me.

3. Thou Shalt Honor Thy Wife with Thy Words

"You shall not misuse the name of the Lord your God"

(Exodus 20:7 NIV).

It is part of the fallen human nature to lose affection and respect for people with whom we become familiar and about whom we gradually begin to speak of irreverently. This command warns us not do this with God. To become careless with the name of God reflects a lack of esteem in which we hold Him. Lack of reverence for God can happen slowly, almost imperceptibly. A little cynicism here, some sarcasm there, and before long He has become smaller in our minds. He is no longer Someone to be awed and respected. The words we use do matter. They reflect our thoughts and emotions towards the person of God.

How this relates to a man's relationship with his wife is that there is no other relationship that a man has which he will be as tempted to take for granted as his relationship with his wife. He will be tempted to treat her with the contempt bred by familiarity.

A Husband of Hesed will treat his wife with a sense of awe and respect in how he speaks *to* her and *of* her. He knows that "reckless words pierce like a sword but the tongue of the wise brings healing" (Proverbs 12:18 NIV). Over and over again, I have had to learn the importance of being careful how I speak to my wife. If I have a sarcastic, flippant attitude my children all too quickly pick it up as well. Words do matter. They can either convey honor and esteem or contempt and disdain. The choice is up to each of us as husbands how we use our words towards our wives.

4. Thou Shalt Be Renewed at Least One Day a Week

"Remember the Sabbath day by keeping it holy"

(Exodus 20:8 NIV).

The typical American male is said to "worship at his work, work at his play and play at his worship." A man's obsession with his work has caused more damage to marriage than perhaps any other factor. Men often look to their jobs to give them the affirmation that they should be receiving first from God and secondly from their family.

Compounding the problem of misplaced worship of work is the phenomenon of men working at their play. Obsessive involvement in sports can take valuable time from the husband-wife relationship. Many men are also addicted to gambling or watching sports on television. I have battled the watching-sports-on-TV addiction. I saw my father and my grandfathers watch sports on the weekends for hours, and I began to watch sports excessively long before I became a father. Like father, like son. The problem for my marriage and me was that for many years it became an addiction that I could not control. I regret the time that could have been spent with family but was squandered.

The Husband of Hesed will see how important it is to have a Sabbath rest, taking one day out of the week where he can nurture his spirit and not squander it on overwork or empty escape. He will lead his wife in commitment to a community of faith where they can worship together as a family and to a caring small group where they can be spiritually replenished. He will make the filling up of his own spiritual tank a priority because he knows that is how he can best give to his wife without the manipulation of giving only to receive in return.

5. Thou Shalt Leave Thy Parents and Cleave to Thy Wife

"Honor your father and your mother so that you may live long in the land the LORD, your God is giving you."

(Exodus 20:12 NIV)

Remember Dan's story? This is the "leave and cleave" principle he applied in the nick of time. It saved his marriage. Notice that the command is to honor, not simply to obey. According to the Bible, when a man marries a woman, he is called to "leave his father and mother and be united to his wife, and the two will become one flesh" (Genesis 2:24, Matthew 19:5 NIV). However, a newly married man finds himself pulled in two directions, both potentially disastrous to his marriage. The first extreme is to see his wife only as some sort of addition to the family to which he already belongs, like an additional daughter for his parents. It may appear to that new husband that he is honoring his parents. But by failing to shift his loyalty from his parents to his new wife, he is in fact dishonoring them by not truly leaving and cleaving. Psychologists call this problem "enmeshment." The other dangerous extreme is "detachment," when a man does as little as possible to treat his parents and his in-laws in a way that is respectful and God honoring.

My marriage lasted exactly one week until I was tested with where my loyalty would lie. Cindy, after the honeymoon was over, got sick, and my dear mother could not understand what was the matter with her. I foolishly went to my wife with the perspective that my mother had a point or two to make about her need to change her attitude. You can guess the outcome of that conversation! It is kind of comical now, but this kind of parental enmeshment in children's lives after marriage is no laughing matter. In the case of my mother, it was not a case of her being wrong and my wife being right; it was about me being loyal to my wife above all.

Leaving and cleaving is difficult work but it is definitely worth it. The husband of Hesed leaves his parents and gently helps his wife shift her loyalty from her parents to their new family by being careful to honor and value both sets of parents. In so doing he partners with the heavenly Father in forming a new family that will uniquely glorify Him while still honoring his and his wife's heritage.

6. Thou Shalt Be The First One to Admit Thou Art at Fault

"You shall not commit murder"

(Exodus 20:13 NIV).

When she was asked if she ever thought of divorcing my grandpa, my Grandma Vi, my father's mother, used to say, "Murder yes, divorce no!" It is almost inconceivable that the same woman a man was once so in love with could become the person he later grows to hate, even wants to destroy. But this is the sad reality of marriage apart from power of confession, repentance, and forgiveness. We live in a world of disposable relationships, divorced or never-married parents, with disowned or never-claimed children and all-too-soon-forgotten grandparents.

In light of this culture of alienation, a Husband of Hesed, when facing inevitable conflict with his wife, must be willing to be the first one to reach out in an effort to reconcile and restore the loving relationship. He must be willing to be the first "to go to the cross." He may be five-percent wrong and his wife ninety-five percent to blame, which is probably not true in most cases. But that does not matter. A husband needs to take it upon himself to "face his five percent," to humble himself, to ask for forgiveness, and then extend forgiveness to his wife.

He needs to recognize that his wife is not the enemy, but the enemy is the sin that lives in both of them. He will be careful not to wound with his words, but he will focus first on taking the log out of his own eye before becoming a "speck-inspector" of his wife.

This is a message I had to learn the hard way during the "8th Year Rash", in our marriage. Ever since that time, whenever I have owned my part in a conflict, our relationship has prospered. An ad shown during the 1960s was intended to teach people about defensive driving. It showed a car, with a person inside, demolished from a head-on accident. The voice in the ad said something like this, "There's ol' _____ in there. He was 'in the right.' Yeah, he was dead right." I have learned that my job is to work on making *things* right, not proving to Cindy that I *am* right…or else like that poor old guy in the mangled vehicle, I will be "dead right."

7. Thou Shalt Focus Thy Sexual Desires upon Thy Wife Alone

"You shall not commit adultery"

(Exodus 20:14 NIV).

Think about it, for generations old farmer John would be holding onto his plough, walking through his field while looking at the back side of a mule or an ox for hours. When he finally returned at night to see his wife she would look pretty good to him in comparison! But consider the barrage of media images bombarding a married man today in the 21st Century beckoning him to be dissatisfied with the wife he has.

Today sexual pleasure, experience, and variety are often exalted above marital faithfulness. Faithfulness to one spouse is seen by many as a puritanical vestige that interferes with individual freedom. The apostle Paul, writing in the First Century, could have been describing 21st Century North Americans when he described his world as, "having lost all sensitivity so as to indulge in every kind of impurity with a continual lust for more" (Ephesians 4:19 NIV).

The Husband of Hesed will pay particular attention to this seventh commandment knowing that in his teaching, Jesus broadened it by equating lustful thoughts toward other women with actual adultery (Matthew 5:28). A faithful husband needs to focus his sexual energy upon his wife alone. "Drink water from your own cistern, draw water from your own well. Rejoice in the wife of your youth, may her breasts satisfy you always" (Proverbs 5:18-19 NIV).

The Husband of Hesed knows that he cannot afford the supposed luxury of indulging in sexual fantasies toward other women. A man who made a great spiritual impact upon me used to say, "I need to guard my heart in this area of purity not because I am a *holy* man but because I am a very *unholy* man." A man keeps morally pure by seeking to live in intimacy with the heavenly Father as well as with his wife. It has been rightly said that the most powerful deterrent to adultery in marriage and to many smaller infidelities, is to see God's fidelity (Hesed) toward us and to seek an intimate relationship with Him.

A husband draws his strength from the faithful, sacrificial hesed of his heavenly Father by making Him Lord of his sex life.

8. Thou Shalt Adequately Provide for Thy Family

"You shall not steal"

(Exodus 20:15 NIV).

It is very possible for a father to provide material needs but steal from his family emotionally. In 21st century North America, the situation many men find themselves in is that materially they are overproviding and yet emotionally they are underproviding for their families. The Bible pointedly says, "Better one handful with tranquillity [emotional provision] than two handfuls with toil and chasing after the wind [emotional barrenness]" (Ecclesiastes 4:6 NIV, parenthetic statements added).

How a husband does this is unique to each individual. As a husband you are to provide more than money and things for your wife and children. You are to be willing to give yourself. Again the Bible cautions, "Do not wear yourself out to get rich, have the wisdom to show restraint" (Proverbs 23:4 NIV). Why restraint? So that a husband can still have some gas in his tank when he arrives home from work.

9. Thou Shalt Not Lie to Thy Wife

"You shall not give false testimony."

(Exodus 20:16 NIV)

Deception can destroy the best of marriages; it all begins with self-deception. A man can deceive himself into believing that he is right and without fault in relating to his wife and children while he pursues some other relationship outside the family. Then, from this self-deception, flows spouse-deception and lying, the kind of cover-up that originated in the fall in the Garden of Eden. The only reason a husband will try to deceive his wife is to cover up his own sin. Trust, once broken, takes much time to be restored.

There have been times when I have not been completely honest with my wife. I have told myself that I am not lying to her, but I am just not giving her the full story. I even, self-righteously in a certain situation, told myself that she "can't handle the truth." Nonsense! There may have been times that I found it wise to wait for the right timing to tell Cindy something, but I am now, more than ever before, committed to total honesty. Anything less breeds distrust.

10. Be Thankful for Thy Wife and The Special Life Thou Hast Together

"You shall not covet your neighbor's house, wife, or anything that belongs to your neighbor"
(Exodus 20:17 NIV).

The roots of the sin of covetousness are planted deeply within the hearts of men and women going right back to the Garden of Eden.

The woman saw that the fruit of the tree was good for food and pleasing to the eye and also desirable for gaining wisdom, so she took some and ate it"

(Genesis 3:6 NIV)

A man's marriage is like a garden where weeds of covetousness constantly sprout up and seek to devour the beauty of that special relationship he has with his wife. We live in a media-saturated world that is constantly seeking to make us feel discontented in order to sell us more products. The temptation will come in many forms, "I wish my wife was prettier, thinner, younger, etc. If only I had married that woman. Why can't my wife be like _____?"

Covetousness thrives where gratitude is absent. Gratitude is God's antidote to covetousness. Gratitude is a conscious choice where you cherish what the heavenly Father has provided you. A Husband of Hesed chooses to practice thanksgiving even when he may not feel like it. The apostle Paul reminds us, "Rejoice in the Lord always. Again I say: Rejoice" (Philippians 4:4 NIV). And later we are reminded, "Through Jesus, therefore, let us continually offer to God a sacrifice of praise-the fruit of lips that confess His name. And do not forget to do good and share with others, for with such sacrifices God is pleased (Hebrews 13:15-16 NIV).

The Husband of Hesed asks the Father to continually protect him from the sin of coveting. He knows his weakness, knows that he needs to repeatedly cry out to the Lord as David did when he prayed, "Search me, O God, and know my heart; test me and know my anxious thoughts. See if there is any offensive way in me, and lead me in the way everlasting (Psalm 139:23-24 NIV).

The Husband of Hesed recognizes that the lie that "grass is greener on the other side" is from the enemy of his marriage. As Dr. James Dobson has been known to say, "the grass on the other side still has to be mowed". A husband accepts that he has been given just what he needs, both in this life and the life to come by an all-wise and all-loving heavenly Father. He is learning that his own and his wife's weaknesses are "divinely designed deficits" that lead him as a husband to depend upon Christ for his strength (2 Corinthians 12:9-10).

The Husband of Hesed is a man who has chosen to faithfully and sacrificially to serve his wife through obedience to God's Word and in dependence upon the Holy Spirit. Loving his wife is the most significant way that he worships God (Romans 12:1) in response to the mystery of the heavenly Father's love for him through the cross of His Son. Through growing in this practical hesed toward his wife, he comes to know more fully the reality of the Father's hesed toward him through Christ. And as he comes to grasp more completely this loyal love of Christ, he is increasingly able to extend that kind of love to his wife, his children, and the world.

A Father's Prayer Of Transformation

Dear Father,

I praise You that You have so wisely designed the relationship between a husband and a wife to picture the relationship between Your Son and His Bride, the Church (Ephesians 5:21-33). This is a mystery that I am in awe of.

I confess, Lord Jesus, that I have either seen my role as one who is to control my wife or as one who retreats in passivity from any conflict. Both are wrong. I am called to be an initiating servant, a Husband of Hesed to faithfully love and serve her and sacrifice myself for her as You did for me (Ephesians 5:25). I all too easily cling to my own rights, desiring to fulfill my own needs. Forgive me, Lord, and teach me to put my wife's needs ahead of my own as we seek to put our marriage under Your Lordship.

I thank You, Father, for the wonderful gift that my wife is to me, my children and to the world. I thank You for the qualities You have given to her that bless me and our children. I also thank You for her weaknesses and the areas in her life that You are still working on. For in those areas I grow in patience, perseverance, and your unconditional love. She is just what I need to become more like Your Son (James 1:1-2).

Father, will You please remind me of all that is at stake in protecting my marriage—for me, my wife, my children, and so many more? Remind me that this relationship isn't just about my wife or me but about You being glorified through this sacred covenant. Will You enable me to lay a foundation for my children and grandchildren of a loving, Christ-centered marriage as an example for them to follow? I submit myself to this holy purpose.

In Jesus' precious name, Amen

(If you are divorced)

Dear Father,

I know that divorce is not Your will. I know that it is a tragedy with many victims. I take responsibility for my part. You know all about that and I thank You for Your complete forgiveness and that there is no condemnation for those who are in Christ Jesus (Romans 8:1). As I live out the painful consequences of what has occurred between my former wife and me, I ask that one of the consequences would not be the passing on of a legacy of divorce to my children and grandchildren. In fact, I ask that You would stop divorce from being a curse passed down my family line. Let it stop with this marriage. I ask for Your mercy in this as I know how painful divorce is and I don't want my children or grandchildren to suffer any more than they have already.

Merciful Father, I ask that You bless my former wife. I only desire the best for her. Bless her as a mother to my children and help us as much as possible to work together in a respectful way for their good. I also ask that You take my brokenness and use it to help the many other men who have gone through the same pain and yet are without You and without hope (2 Corinthians 1:3-4). Will You please use what the enemy has intended for evil and work it for good in my life, my former wife's life, and my children's lives (Genesis 50:20)? I believe You desire to do this! I thank You that You have for all of us plans for blessing, to give us all a future and a hope (Jeremiah 29:11).

In Jesus' precious name, Amen.

Chapter 2

TEAMING INTENTIONALLY

"Two are better than one, because they have a good return for their work: If one falls down his friend can help him up. But pity the man who falls and has no one to help him up! Also, if two lie down together, they will keep warm. But how can one keep warm alone? Though one may be overpowered, two can defend themselves. A cord of three strands is not quickly broken"
(Ecc. 4:9-12 NIV).

The Danger of NOT Working as a Team

On September 11, 2001, members of the al-Qaida international terror network caught the United States of America flat-footed. The September 11 Commission unanimously declared in its final report:

"The institutions charged with protecting our borders, civil aviation and national security, did not understand how grave this threat could be and did not adjust their policies, plans and practices to deter or defeat it."[1]

The report revealed that various FBI agents came across important clues to the unfolding al-Qaida plot but they could not get that information through the walls separating various agencies. The enemy had evolved but the U.S. defense apparatus had not. All of the key components for discovery were in place but the agencies were not working together, communicating, pooling their resources. We all know now the loss of lives and the impact upon our nation and the world that this failure to partner together caused.

There is a corresponding need for a father to team with his children's mother in the task of parenting. Fathers AND mothers are both charged with raising their children, and together they provide the greatest possible protection against Satan and his forces of spiritual darkness, the enemies of their children's souls. But if a father and mother do not communicate with each other and learn to adjust to the enemy's threats to their children, the results can be as disastrous as 9/11.

In a recent study, University of Washington expert marriage researcher, Dr. John Gottman, tracked eighty-two newlywed couples for four to six years. He discovered that a married couple's inability to adjust to a new child and equitably share the changing workload spells danger in a marriage.

Of the eighty-two couples, forty-three became parents. Of these, two-thirds cited marital dissatisfaction within three years of the baby's birth. The dissatisfaction was caused by the fact that they experienced a breakdown in communication, an inability to resolve conflicts, difficulty in negotiating responsibilities, and philosophical differences.[2]

Much like the U.S. government before 9/11, married couples are getting caught unprepared when children enter the family. They are not able to adjust to the evolving challenge to marital unity that raising children presents. The following needs to be emphasized: For parents, learning to work as a team in their parenting is essential for successfully raising their children. This parental teamwork is also vital for building a lasting marriage. PARENTAL TEAMWORK IS ABOUT BOTH BUILDING A STRONG MARRIAGE AND BUILDING STRONG KIDS!

The Power of the Husband—Wife Team

There is a clear biblical mandate for both a husband and wife to work as a team in their parenting. The command goes all the way back to God's intention in creation and applies to all people. "So God created man in his own image, in the image of God he created him, male and female he created them. God blessed them and said to them, 'Be fruitful and increase in number, fill the earth and subdue it" (Genesis 1:27-28 NIV).

The triune God decided to reveal Himself not through one man alone, not through one woman alone, not through any two people together, but through a man and a woman together. A married couple displays His image. The unity in the diversity of this unique relationship reveals God's personhood like nothing else on this earth. It isn't any wonder that the enemy's forces have invested so much energy and so many resources in their attempt to destroy the institution of marriage in our culture.

The first couple was to live out their God-image-bearing glory through having children and ruling righteously over them and all creation. This was to be a team project — not just something given only to mothers or only to fathers. Of course the fall of man marred this picture, but never really shattered it. Every single father or single mother I have known over the years, though heroic in raising children on their own, has told me a story of the painful realization that they were never designed to do it alone.

Throughout Scripture it is taken for granted that the ideal way for children to be raised is with a father-mother team cooperating with one another, complementing one another. In the Bible we see God's heart for the fatherless because He knows that children raised by a single woman or a single man are extremely vulnerable and need a community of faithful men and women around them to provide what is lacking (James 1:27).

Moms and dads parent differently and that is part of the Heavenly Father's wonderfully wise plan of completion in two becoming one. King Solomon commanded the sons of Israel, "Listen my son to your father's instruction and do not forsake your mother's teaching" (Proverbs 1:8 NIV). And the apostle Paul in his letter to the Thessalonians used images both of a father and mother to express how he cared for them. First he used the picture of a mother: "We were gentle among you like a mother caring for her little children." (1 Thessalonians 2:7 NIV). He then switched to the picture of a father's love, "For you know that we dealt with each of you as a father deals with his own children, encouraging, comforting and urging you to live lives worthy of God who calls you into His kingdom and glory" (1 Thessalonians 2:11-12 NIV).

Besides the biblical mandate there are benefits of parental partnership that can be readily observed.

WHAT DADS CONTRIBUTE TO THE PARENTAL TEAM

Dads Play Differently

A 1999 Harvard University study by Eleanor E. Maccoby showed that seventy percent of the time that a father and infant played together it was action-oriented. During their playtime with their mother only four percent of their play was strongly physical.[2]

In my family, when my kids were younger, we called dad-kid play time "rough-up time." I would wrestle with and tickle the kids, play hide-and-go-seek, throw them around, etc. By doing this with my children, I taught them a healthy balance between proper caution and aggression. I taught them that there are appropriate boundaries when roughhousing. A child who has no benefit of this kind of play will either become overly aggressive, not understanding those boundaries, or will become timid, afraid of any rough-and-tumble kind of behavior.

Dads Push the Limits While Moms Remind Dads That There ARE Limits!

Go to a playground sometime and observe both a mother and a father playing with their children. Chances are that Dad will be the one pushing the swing to go higher and faster while Mom will probably be in the background ever reminding her husband, "Be careful, not too high, remember he's only two." The child is probably laughing gleefully and Dad will reply, "Look, he's having fun; he's not crying." Mom will counter, "No, that's not a look of having fun; that's the look of terror in his eyes. He is too frightened to cry." And so it goes.

Children need both Mom and Dad to strike a healthy balance in parenting by working together. If Dad isn't there, the children may grow up excessively timid, and if Mom isn't there those children may never survive childhood to see adulthood!

Dads Communicate Differently Than Moms

Men and women communicate to their children differently. A father tends to be more direct and to the point. He relies on body language to get his message across. A mother, on the other hand, tends to be more verbal encouraging, coaxing her child. When a child grows up in a home where both parents are actively parenting, he will grow up with the social advantage of knowing two languages, not English and Japanese, but male and female. He will be better able to communicate in his adult world to both men and women equally.

Dads Discipline Differently Than Moms

Educational psychologist Carol Gilligan has discovered through her research that mothers and fathers discipline their children in complementary ways, emphasizing different essentials to their children. Fathers tend to stress justice, fairness, and duty. Mothers will generally be more sympathetic, caring, and helpful to their children. Fathers are more truth-based, while mothers emphasize the importance of relationship. Neither Mom nor Dad is a complete, balanced expression of healthy discipline in himself or herself.[3] These findings confirm God's Word (Genesis 1:27-28). Husband and wife need each other to paint a balanced picture of what the Bible teaches us about God's character.

Dads Prepare Their Children for Life Differently Than Moms

Men tend to prepare their children for life by looking forward with "pro-vision." They see the challenges and obstacles ahead and try to prepare them much as a drill sergeant prepares young recruits for upcoming battles. Men can be tough because they know that the world is tough and their children need to be prepared to face it. Picture in your mind a child with an arrow going right from him towards a circle. In that circle are the challenges that lie ahead, things like finding a job, relating to the opposite sex, being ready to try out for the soccer team and dealing with a bully. That is how a father will tend to see his role.

Conversely, mothers tend to prepare their children for the world by trying to protect them from the world. Moms will tend to see their children in the middle of the circle with many arrows (sickness, strangers, unhealthy risks etc.) trying to penetrate that bubble. They simply want their children to survive their childhood. That little detail about keeping them safe is something we dads need a little reminder about now and then!

Dads Teach Their Sons to Respect Women

My wife, Cindy, has the gift of discernment. For example, when we spend time with certain people she will pick up that a man has a problem respecting women. "What do you mean?" I usually lamely reply. "How can you see that in just a few minutes?" She has yet to be proven wrong, I have to admit. Being a man I have a distinct blindness to this problem. But many women, like my wife, can quickly sense it.

If a husband/father is dominant, overpowering his wife in the parenting role, treating her as just another child to keep under control, children will grow up to view women as unequal to men. If a father is passively detached and gives over parenting to the mother, children will learn to disrespect men and resent women. Either way, children can have gender issues that could have been avoided if their father had simply partnered with his wife by assuming his proper parenting role.

Dads Offer the Greatest Encouragement to Moms

It is vitally important that a husband encourage his wife in her mothering role. If a husband does not affirm his wife in her parenting whom else will? Will the children? I am working with my kids to help them become more appreciative of their mother, but this takes time…like twenty years or more! Certainly they do not give her the daily feedback she needs. It is sporadic and delayed at best

How about encouragement by parents or in-laws? Sometimes comments made by extended family members are the most hurtful. Cindy and I have seen couples, convinced that they need to apply corporal punishment to their children, accused by their own relatives of abusing their children. More common than that, however, is a lack of any involvement or closeness by extended families. Families generally are just too far away, geographically spread apart, and relationally fragmented to be of significant encouragement to a mother in the trenches.

How about a wife's friends, neighbors, or co-workers? They may offer an occasional word of encouragement, but many women today have swallowed the lie that motherhood is not a high and noble calling. People usually offer little inspiration to a wife who is committed to be a "stay-at-home Mom," or one who works part time in order to be more available to her family.

Does the media provide her encouragement? It seems that all media is united to paint a picture for mothers that only discourages and creates self-doubt. The obsession with eternal romance, youth, sexual freedom, external beauty, status, power, and success all work to downplay the essential role of nurturer that a mother should play in the family and society.

What does your wife give to you free of charge? Besides what you are thinking right at this moment (I KNOW, I'm a guy!). Think about what she contributes to the parenting of your children. It may be helpful to consider this in terms of three categories: traits, talents, and tasks. She has certain valuable traits that most likely supply areas where you may be weak as a parent. These traits are qualities such as patience, kindness, or a serving spirit. She also has talents that compliment yours. These talents may be her ability to organize, solve problems, give counsel, or decorate. Then there are just plain tasks, the things she does week in and week out that become expected, such as cooking, cleaning, shopping, and carpooling.

Consider the fact that your wife contributes her traits and talents and performs her tasks every day for you and your children without cost. There is a "blinding flash of the obvious (BFO)" for you. A husband may still protest, "Yeah, she does those things, but I bust my butt at work to provide for her and she doesn't seem to appreciate that as much as she should."

There are three things that need to be said in response to that. First, chances are that a husband will receive more affirmation from his work than a wife will receive in the home. This is not always the case, but it usually is.

Second, there is a cute little story that illustrates the difference between mothers and fathers when it comes to parental sacrifice. A chicken and a pig got together one day and the chicken said to the pig, "You know, it would be nice to do something special for our farmer family for providing us this nice barn. How about we provide them a breakfast of bacon and eggs tomorrow morning." The pig thought and said, "That's a nice gesture, but the only problem is that for you that would be a contribution, but for me that would be a real sacrifice."

The wife is often like the "sacrificial pig" and the husband's role resembles the "contributing chicken." All illustrations have their limitations (moms aren't pigs!) but the point here is that mothers truly sacrifice their bodies through pregnancy, nursing, and nurturing while we fathers have made our "contribution" by impregnating them. A woman is very vulnerable when she becomes a mother. She is depending upon her husband for herself and her children in ways that her husband does not need to depend upon her. It is a time when she is in great need for affirmation, support, and understanding.

Third, it is the special calling of the husband to be the initiating servant in the family, loving his wife as Christ initiated His love for us (Ephesians 5:22-33). The husband is not called to be the responder but the initiator. In my opinion that defines a husband's headship. This means he is the one who provides the affirmation that she needs even at times when she cannot respond back in ways that he would desire.

I grieve for the many times I have failed to value and cherish my wife for her mothering role of our children, for her serving our family through her parenting. And I know that I am not the only father or husband who has failed to appreciate his wife in this role. I cannot turn the clock back but I can choose to make it a present and future priority to appreciate my wife in her role as my children's mom.

Husbands often fail to see this "blinding flash of the obvious" and do not affirm their wives in the parenting role by consistently encouraging them.

DADS' BARRIERS TO OVERCOME TO PARTNER IN PARENTING

Poor Modeling by His Dad

Like father, like son. For the most part I had good modeling from my father when it came to learning to appreciate my mother's sacrifice. His father taught him and he taught me to appreciate what my mother did for us. I have sought to build upon this strength.

However, there was another factor at work in our home when I was growing up. I had a father who had learned to delegate much of the day-to-day family operations, including discipline, to my mother. His father was absent from the home for most of his childhood out of necessity since he owned a heavy construction business. Grandpa Floyd delegated the discipline of my dad and his three brothers to my Grandma Vi, who was no pushover! I felt her wrath a couple of times when she and Grandpa would house sit for my parents and I learned the hard way that you did not mess with that lady!

When my father began his role as a father he was called up from the reserves into the Korean War as a pilot. Later he traveled much throughout the week building a national restaurant chain. So he delegated discipline and many of the day–to-day details of raising a family to my mother. My mother was not as tough as my grandmother was in her discipline and, though she was a wonderful mother, our family could have been stronger in the discipline area if she had been.

I believe that fathers will default to what they learned from their father or father-figure if there is no conscious choice to make a change. Like father, like son. A good example of that principle in action in my life is when there is an issue regarding discipline of one of our children. I wonder why Cindy can not just handle it herself. And I do not run a big construction business as my grandather did where I am gone for weeks at a time. I am not off to war or building a restaurant chain as my dad was. I am seeking to partner with my wife in raising our children and helping other families as we do that. Yet I still, often *emotionally* respond in ways that my grandpa or father probably would, wanting to delegate the responsibility rather than share it. For them it was the only practical response to their situations. But for me, "Mr. Fathering Forum," it certainly is not!

There is the story of a young mother who was at a large family gathering and she was putting a roast into the oven. Someone asked her, "Why do you cut off the ends of the roast and waste all that meat before you put it into the oven?" Her response was, "That's how my mother taught me to do it." The young mother, kind of bothered by this, went to her mother and asked her why she had taught her to cut off the ends of the roast. Her mother replied that it was because that's how her mother had taught her to do it. Now the young mother was really curious. Her grandmother was at the gathering and she asked her how this habit of cutting off the ends of roasts got started. Her grandma replied, "That's easy, dearie. That was the only way it would fit into my pan."

Fathers carry on many similar automatic responses that may have made some sense a couple of generations ago but now are actually harmful to their families. It is easy to see where my reluctance to partner in discipline comes from. I admit that I naturally want to take the path of least resistance and that is simply part of my self-centered sinfulness. But there is also something else at play here, something generational. Like grandfather, like father. Like father, like son.

The Desire to Avoid Conflict with His Wife

A husband and wife come to parenting from different backgrounds and have different emphases, different strengths and weaknesses, which all have the potential to cause conflict. Conflict can be handled either by respectfully working toward solutions and compromises that respect both partners or avoided because that means work and it takes time. It is good to remember that "in relationships fast is slow and slow is fast." Today, with so many families under so much stress, husbands are choosing to avoid parental interaction because of the risk of opening up more areas of conflict. This is not good, nor does it resolve any of the issues.

Overreaction to His Needs not Being Met

Just about every study or survey ever done shows that a husband's perceived number one need is having a satisfying sexual relationship with his wife. What happens often is that when a baby comes, the wife's identity is swallowed up in her motherhood role. Her sexual desire diminishes-at least for a time. Her desire to be touched is usually lessened as she is groped and pulled at all day by little junior. Before children, a woman may have been an eager sexual responder to her husband's romantic advances. But being a mother changes things as she struggles to adapt to her new dual role of wife *and* mother.

A natural response is for the husband to feel rejected and to retaliate in ways that can be hurtful. One way to "strike back" for a husband is to not help with parenting tasks. "Why encourage her to continue to do the very thing that seems to be keeping her from meeting my needs?" he foolishly reasons. If he seeks to affirm her as a mother when his needs are not being met, he feels as though he is rewarding bad behavior. He has anger, jealousy, and deep resentment, and he thinks that the best thing for him to do is to detach and withdraw.

Taking His Wife's Parental Commitment for Granted

Although this is closely related to the previous point there is a difference. I could never understand why Cindy got so upset when she heard me refer to it as "baby-sitting' when I had to watch the kids when she went out for a while. I now understand why that really touched a nerve. What husbands communicate to their wives when they say that is simply that this parenting is YOUR job, and for me it is just a once and a while thing to relieve you when you need a break from YOUR job. I wish I could say that I never had this attitude, but I have. The attitude that causes me the most anger in my family is when I see my kids act as if they are entitled to something or when the do not show any gratitude. But then I am reminded that this is what I often express to Cindy, the woman who has sacrificed so much for me and our children.

To facilitate parental partnership, a husband who is committed to team with his wife in parenting can do some specific things.

What Dads Can DO to Encourage Parental Partnership

Initiate Regular Interaction about Parenting Challenges

In retrospect, we could have avoided much of the pain of our early years of marriage if I had been initiating regular times for us to sit down and talk about what Cindy was going through as a young mother. But I was totally blind to how I had become detached and how it affected her sense of self-esteem as a wife and mother. I was not empathizing with what she was going through and she felt isolated and alone.

Becoming a mother is a disorienting time for a woman and she needs a husband to help her process it all and demonstrate to her how much she is appreciated. I have learned that Cindy does not need for me to "fix" the situation or solve her problem. She just needs to process her feelings a little bit with me. That takes the pressure off.

Regularly Affirm your Wife's Parental Contributions

We husbands forget that our wives need regular, consistent affirmation in their parenting. Their sacrificial efforts need to be constantly appreciated and acknowledged. If your wife is a follower of Christ she should look to the heavenly Father for her primary affirmation. But even then the husband is the primary human means of conveying God's affirmation to her. If regular affirmation was not modeled in your home growing up, it may seem awkward to you. But make an effort to begin to recognize the wonderful things that your wife does for your family and verbalize appreciation.

Pray Together for Your Family

There is nothing as powerful as prayer to unify a couple and build partnership, because it is then a three-way partnership with God, the heavenly Father. As together you lift the concerns of your family to Him, the bonds between father and mother are strengthened. As prayers are answered, your faith in God as your Provider also grows and gives stability despite changing circumstances.

A Father's Prayer of Transformation

Dear Father,

Will you remind me that my marriage and my partnership is a picture of the triune relationship You have with the Son and the Spirit? Remind me that there is so much at stake in my wife and me loving and working together in raising our children. Father, don't let our love for one another grow cold but fan it into flame by continually reminding us of Your love for us both (I John 3:1-3).

Father, forgive me for taking my wife for granted. She gives so much to me and the family. Make me a servant to her and the kids. Teach me to move away from any tendencies I may have inherited from my father that keep me from wholeheartedly teaming up with my wife. In the name of Your dear Son, Amen.

SECTION 2

PREPARING YOUR CHILD FOR LIFE—MEETING PHYSICAL NEEDS

There is something about the challenge of meeting our children's physical needs that has the potential of bringing us into direct contact with our need of the heavenly Father. Whether it be providing for, protecting, disciplining, or teaching our kids, we come to face our inadequacy to the task and our need and our children's need for Another Father. These challenges also bring up issues with our own fathers that before we were fathers ourselves did not seem as relevant. For example, suddenly when it comes to issues around his work, a father can feel more strongly the influence of his dad, both good and bad.

David found that when he was to become a father he began to rely upon God in ways that marriage without children did not foster in him. As he worked and trusted in the heavenly Father's provision, he also became aware of the influence that his father still had upon him. He measured himself against his father in unfavorable ways. He also began to fear that his work would pull him away from his wife and child as his dad's work seemed to emotionally distance him from the family.

Let's hear David's story in his own words:

I had been a Christian since I was five years old. I grew up in a Christian family, but when I left home around age eighteen, I went my own way. When my wife and I decided to start having kids, my biggest concern was how I was going to be able to provide for my family. We were pretty strapped financially and I was wondering how we were going to do this. Also, the process of having children made me think more spiritually. It was then that we started going back to church.

It was kind of funny because there was a church in our neighborhood and it was the last place I thought we would be going. But having kids brought me back to my knees. We started going to that church. I think that God started to talk to both my wife and me. My wife wasn't even a Christian at that time. We got started with a prayer life. There were a lot of other things going on in my life that were not right.

From there we began to see prayers answered. I began to see God as the Good Shepherd and us being His sheep. I had strayed. God didn't just bring me back in a punishing sort of way but He brought me back into the fold in a gentle way.

Just about the time we went back to church, we got involved in a Bible study about how to manage our money. We hadn't done that very well. We hadn't needed to worry about our money before, when we were both working and without kids. As we started to get into the Bible study, we began to give more. This is still a struggle. About the time we became pregnant, I began to work for my wife's jewelry business. From month to month we didn't see how we were going to be able to make ends meet. Sometimes on the last day of the month we would make a sale and get our bills paid. We were beginning to tithe at that time. We had to give sometimes when that money could have gone to pay the bills.

Lately I have thought about my relationship with my dad. He gave me a strong work ethic, almost to a fault. I don't think my father was truly grounded in his faith. Recently my family found out that my father had an ongoing affair with another woman. This had been going on since I was nine years old.

We found this out about a year and a half ago. As I look back on my life I can see certain things about my father that start to make sense. He wasn't available for me in certain ways. In a lot of ways I don't think I am bitter. As far as self-esteem is concerned, it is a wonder I was able to grow up as I did. I had self-esteem problems."

Meeting challenges as fathers to meet our children's material needs brings up issues with our own earthly fathers. More importantly this drives us into the arms of the heavenly Father.

Chapter 3

PROVIDING ADEQUATELY

"If anyone does not provide for his relatives, and especially for his immediate family, he has denied the faith and is worse than an unbeliever"

(1 Tim. 5:8 NIV).

Provision and Distorted Heavenly Father Images

A father's provision for his family makes a definite spiritual imprint upon his children's view of how God provides for them.

In other words, the way a father approaches his providing role can influence his child to see God, the provider, in a certain way. If a father is neglectful, lazy, or sporadic in his work, he will inadvertently communicate to his children that God the Father, is a Person who cannot be depended upon to meet their needs. What is seen reveals what is unseen.

If a father, on the other extreme, is a man driven in his work so much that it emotionally takes him away from his home, then he portrays a God who provides many "presents" but not much "presence." In other words, he projects an image of a God who substitutes giving lots of "stuff" in the place of giving Himself in genuine relationship with His children.

If you grew up in a home that struggled financially you may continue to struggle to trust the heavenly Father to meet your needs. You may feel a "disconnect" from the objective knowledge that God loves you and the practical physical expression of that love. You may have a hard time believing that "every good and perfect gift is from above coming down *from the Father* of heavenly lights" (James 1:17 NIV). You may view God as not quite willing or able to meet your needs now.

If, on the other hand, you come from a family that had plenty of material things, you may feel that your father sacrificed his "presence" for "presents."

If your father provided abundantly at the cost of relationship, then chances are you will not feel the heavenly Father's love behind everything He provides for you. You may see the heavenly Father's *hand* but not His *heart* behind the hand. This would be a natural conclusion to draw since just as your father often was "invisible" by his absence, your heavenly Father is an invisible Spirit even in His presence.

How were *you* fathered in the area of material provision? The question each of us needs to ask is, "How has that impacted my view of my heavenly Father?"

A Paradox of Being a Provider

It is a high privilege for a man to be the primary provider for his family. It touches the very core of a man's made-in-God's-image dignity, that of being a creator himself. It takes him back to the Garden of Eden when God chose to co-labor with him in making the earth beautiful and by allowing him to name his animals. God could have bypassed man, but He chose to partner with him, making work a cooperative venture. For man to co-create with God reflects the height of his dignity and design.

However, there is a reason that a man is fraught with so many challenges as he provides for his family. After Adam and Eve sinned in the garden, God gave both the man and woman a curse. For man his curse had to do with his work; for woman it had to do with childbearing. God said to Adam, who had previously fully enjoyed his job as head gardener of Eden, "Cursed is the ground because of you; through painful toil you will eat of it all the days of your life. It will produce thorns and thistles for you and you will eat the plants of the field. By the sweat of your brow you will eat your food until you return to the ground, since from it you were taken; for dust you are and to dust you will return" (Genesis 3;17-19 NIV).

So after Adam sinned, work would be hard. To provide for one's family is not easy. It is hard work full of frustrations (thorns, and thistles). Here we are in the 21st century with all of the technology and labor-saving devices and yet we have not avoided the curse. Work is still hard. Men and women are working longer in America today than ever before-and are under more stress.

There is perhaps no other aspect of your fatherhood that will stir up more issues and bring more temptations for you than providing for your family. In working to provide for a family a man's expectations are very high. But together with the dignity imparted to him all the way back in the Garden of Eden he experiences echoes of the curse. This makes for a strange combination of opposite emotions—high expectations (hopes that work will be fulfilling) and high frustrations (the reality that in a fallen world that work is just plain hard).

It is important to remember that every man's father faced similar temptations in this area. And as he faced his temptations, he, being a sinful man, inevitably wounded his son in the process. When a son becomes a father himself the challenge of providing for his family can open up those old wounds that were never healed.

But there is a blessing hidden within this curse. It is in this part of a father's provider identity, perhaps more than any other area, that a man is most apt to turn to Another Father, the heavenly Father, through His Son, Jesus. Just listen in on a group of men who are supporting and praying for each other and you will hear those men ask for prayer for their jobs. This role stretches a man to turn to outside help.

Temptations Facing Providers

There are at least five temptations facing a providing father:

- Escapism – I refuse to accept any responsibility to provide for my family
- Workaholism - "I can never do enough"
- Perfectionism - "I can never do well enough"
- Careerism – "I can never be significant enough"
- Materialism- "I can never possess enough"

Escapism—"I refuse to take responsibility for providing for my family"

There is something shaming, belittling, and scary for a child to grow up with the knowledge that his or her father does not provide for material needs. The father may in fact care, but he is struggling with an addiction or involved in a vicious cycle that he feels helpless to break. To children the reasons do not matter, but the results do. All they understand is that Dad does not provide. This hit home to me one summer when I took my second trip to Nicaragua with Agros, a Christian development agency that works with the poor in Latin America. A 13-year-old named Julio, whom I came to know the previous year as a happy gregarious boy, had suddenly changed. He was now mean and angry and very difficult to deal with. What I found out is that his father was a German worker who had previously sent money from Germany to help support him. But during the time between our previous visit and this time his father had stopped sending money. This was not only devastating materially but it was clearly wounding emotionally to Julio.

The book of Proverbs gives many warnings to the young man trying to escape the responsibility of productive contribution. The ways of escape are excessive sleep or plain laziness (6:10-11.10:5, 24:33-34) , overindulgence in drink (or drug addiction) (31:6-7) , chasing financial fantasies (gambling) (12:11), pursuing get-rich-quick schemes (13:11), generally making excuses for not working (15:19), neglecting work as a life priority (26:15) and pursuing illicit sexual relationships (chapters 5-7, 31:3).

With all of these warnings about NOT providing, it is important to note that the wisdom of Proverbs gives a warning about the dangers of another extreme that we need to address. "Do not wear yourself out to get rich; have the wisdom to show restraint. Cast but a glance at riches, and they are gone, for they will surely sprout wings and fly off to the sky like an eagle" (Proverbs 23:4-5 NIV). The following temptations for a father relate to an overindulgence in work that will actually cause harm to his family.

"Workaholism"—"I can never do enough"

Now as we look at this extreme, when work takes fathers away from their families, there are four overlapping areas to keep in mind. Today's society has coined this as "workaholism," or addiction to work. Workaholism has to do with the value one puts on his work as well as the quantity of his work. "I can never do enough," is the workaholic's lament in the workplace and in his home.

A grown son who had a father with this tendency and who is now a father himself will likely struggle with the same temptation. Like father, like son. Despite his most solemn vow to "not be like dad" in this area, he will often find himself doing the same kinds of things his father did. He will stay at work away from the family too long and when at home he will likely be unable to give his family anything close to his very best.

For this man's father, his work may have been his "drug of choice" to numb his pain, and he most likely learned these tendencies from his father. Then add to this the fact that today overwork is a socially-acceptable and even encouraged "drug." One can see why this is such a powerful temptation to deal with. Many companies are renowned for their workaholic culture that rewards and advances those who are "willing to pay the price." I live in Redmond, Washington, the home of Microsoft Corporation, a company that prides itself to be a workaholic culture. Do not let the casual attire fool you! This company has influenced the work culture of the entire Northwest region of the U.S.

And what makes this pull so powerful is the workaholic receives great affirmation from others outside of the home. In order for this need for affirmation to continue to be met, the man must keep working. As in drinking saltwater, the more he drinks the thirstier he becomes. He never can receive quite enough satisfaction or affirmation from coworkers, clients, or his boss. He is restless and driven. The only relief he can find is in going back to work. When he works he feels the most alive and valuable. He is no longer behaving like a human being but rather he has become a "human doing."

The workaholic alienates himself from his family as most of his time is spent away from the home. Even when he is home he is "not home" or emotionally present. As Reba McIntyre writes in her song, "The Greatest Man I Never Knew," about an emotionally spent father, "everything he gave us took everything he had."

Perfectionism—"I can never do well enough"

Many sons have grown up with fathers (and mothers!) who gave them the feeling that no matter what they did as a child, it was never done well enough. These sons probably did not realize that their fathers were often made to feel the same way by their fathers. Like father, like son.

A son growing up with this message hanging over him is haunted by the feeling that no matter what he does in providing for his family, it is never adequate. He is robbed of the contentment, the divinely granted satisfaction, of accomplishing a job well done. Whatever he does cannot ever meet the impossible standard in his mind of unattainable perfection.

The perfectionist carries this workplace measuring stick right into his home and makes his wife and children feel the very same anxiety of not measuring up that he feels. He is miserable himself and projects his misery upon his own family. Tragically, these are the very ones he loves the most! The people he desires to draw to himself, he drives away.

The role of provider can tempt a father to strive so hard at work and strive so hard at home that it causes family members to feel that they are constantly being judged, criticized, and evaluated. In short, he creates a home atmosphere that is unsafe and threatening.

Careerism—"I can never be significant enough"

A father faces the temptation of "careerism" when he sees his work as a viable means of getting him a greater sense of his own importance through greater power and control over his life and the lives of others. He develops "tunnel vision" about his career and his advancement. His progress in his career becomes the only consideration in his decision making. Such a man begins to see his work as a tool to be used for his benefit. The National Center For Fathering has discovered through their research that a man feels the lowest satisfaction in his fathering role during his children's teen years. It is interesting that many choose to go into the "sprint mode" in their career at this time when they feel they are losing power and influence at home. It is not just a coincidence that when a man feels his influence with his teens (and intimacy with his wife) is waning he gravitates back into his career.

Tragically, it is when his children hit their adolescent years that an involved father is most needed. This is also a time when the husband-wife relationship is very vulnerable. And then there are the many couples who choose to dissolve their marriages after they have raised the kids and they become "empty nesters." Couples still stay married for the kids' sake—until they leave the home.

Of course, there is nothing wrong with a father mapping out a career path. In fact, the book of Proverbs repeatedly commends the man who plans ahead. But the danger exists when a man's career is his *only* consideration, when he minimizes in importance the needs of his wife and children or, worse, when he completely ignores them.

For men who are all caught up in careerism, it is "all about them." *Their* power, *their* position, *their* prestige are the most important things in their lives. Just as perfectionism and workaholism spill into the home life, when fathers are caught in the trap of careerism they often see their home as just another place for them to be served. They expect their wife and children to do as they say and not give them any resistance. Naturally we all want to see our children obey and behave, but children of careerists often "obey on the outside, but rebel on the inside." Children are very perceptive. They can see into our hearts and know when their father is being selfish and self-serving. They learn to not truly respect their father when they see him only as a man who wants to be served at home.

Often an adult son who has unresolved issues with his father will be lured into careerism in order to attempt to gain the approval that escaped him as a child. This is a tragic misplacement of focus. Rather than working to meet his family's needs, he uses his work as a tool to meet his own unmet needs that are rooted in a wounded relationship with his father. The sad thing is that the son's father, who did not provide affirmation earlier when his son was young, is no more likely to later grant approval now that his son is successful in his chosen vocation.

Materialism—"I can never possess enough"

This is a lie that speaks seductively to the father in his heart. It says, "You know if you just made a little more money or were able to afford _____(fill in the blank), then you would be really doing your job as provider for your family." Maybe it is a larger house or a newer car or a more expensive vacation, but it is always something just out of one's grasp.

We are all bombarded with advertising messages that hammer away at our resistance with the message, "You and your family *need* just a little bit more," What is unsaid is that having more of material things often creates less of the immaterial things, the intangible things such as having time to spend together, time to build deeper relationships in the family, time to strengthen the home ties.

The more things we own, the more things potentially own us. We will have more "stuff" that will need to be taken care of. And have you ever noticed that the more rich we become the more impoverished we can become in other areas of life? A few of the things that extra spendable income provides are an increased opportunity to eat out at restaurants, a greater ability to take part in special programs for the children, and a chance to travel more. But what does this do to the time that a family needs just to "hang out" together or to eat meals together at home? And having more income can mean accumulating more debt, which creates unseen stresses within the home that the wife and children will inevitably feel. Besides this, children who receive too much too soon often lose their sense of appreciation. They forfeit the ability to delay gratification of their desires and are stifled in the development of a healthy work ethic.

Again, the unresolved issues a grown son may have with his father can impact his ability to fight this temptation. If his father did not make a man feel important as a child, this grown son can use things, or symbols of status or success, in order to bolster his feelings of significance. He often makes his own children feel just as overlooked as his father made him feel. Or, if his father was not a reliable provider, he may overcompensate by falling into the foolish trap of believing that an extremely large income and accumulation of things is needed to undo the supposed damage done to him by his under-providing father.

The key to a father's being an effective provider for his family is consistency. A man can do no better than to humbly do his work the best that he can, serving his boss or his customers/clients as if he is serving the Lord Himself (Colossians 3:22-24). It is not about getting rich and providing our family their every want. Rather, we are in a partnership with the heavenly Father to provide for our family's *needs*-not their every want.

Turning Away from the "Isms"

I believe that the all-wise, all-loving, all-compassionate heavenly Father allows these temptations to be a means of blessing us and drawing us to Himself. As the apostle Paul writes, "And we know that in all things God works for the good of those who love him, who have been called according to his purpose. For those God foreknew he also predestined to be conformed to the likeness of his Son" (Romans 8:28-29a NIV).

It has been my experience, and that of a growing number of fathers, that the temptations the providing father faces become the pathways to finding a gracious, compassionate heavenly Father's provision. That is what David's story is all about. I have also had to battle with each of these temptations to one degree or another. For me, I have found they have been avenues for me to come to know the Father's heart in greater clarity. The heavenly Father knows that in our human weakness we will tend not to pursue Him passionately unless we come to a felt need in our lives. Even though God Himself does not tempt, He will use the temptation to draw us to Himself.

The Escape from Escapism

The way of repentance for a man caught up in neglect of provision (escapism) is to simply begin to embrace work head on. My good friend Marvin Charles has turned his life around from being a crack cocaine addict to a man who is responsibly providing for his family. One of the keys to his transformation was that he simply held a steady job. It wasn't a prestigious, high-paying job but it was a job that required him to show up and give his best from 9 to 5. Marvin became a reliable employee and developed a track record of trustworthiness. He and his wife, Jeanett, have since founded D.A.D.S. (Divine Alternatives For Dads Services). They can tell story after story of fathers who have transformed lives. These men were once addicted, hopeless men separated from their children, but are now productive, responsibly meeting their financial obligations to their children. These dads are often tempted to go back to selling drugs for a quick infusion of easy money, but through the support of Marvin and other men they are able to stay on the right course. This is true repentance that blesses children and builds family legacies.

Working Free of Workaholism

The heavenly Father's provision for the father who struggles with the temptation of workaholism is available through His Son, Jesus Christ. One of the toughest things for a workaholic to do is to say "No" to people who are counting on him to meet a need that he is especially suited to meet. This kind of request pushes all of the workaholic's buttons.

The Bible records an amazing scene in Capernaum during Jesus' earthly ministry when He decided to spend some quality time with His Father after a long, busy day and evening of teaching and healing. The disciples came to him with an attitude that all but said, "You are in real demand here. This is where you are being productive. You are being counted upon to stay and continue your work here."

But Jesus was not going to be swayed and governed by others' expectations or the need to finish every task that was before His eyes in Capernaum. He simply followed the Father, doing His will. And after spending this "Daddy Time," He clearly knew that it was appropriate to pull up stakes and move on to other places. Imagine! He was going to leave tasks unfinished and some people he cared about very disappointed.

The most liberating prayer in the Bible for a father who is caught up in the bondage of workaholism is Jesus' prayer to the Father at the very end of His earthly ministry. He said, "Father I have completed the work that You gave Me to do" (John 17:4 NIV).

Thousands of people had still not heard of Him, many others had not been touched or healed by Him and yet He knew that He had completed the work that the Father gave Him to do. The Heavenly Father is the One who gives each of His sons work to do. He is also the One who says, "Do not wear yourself out trying to get rich, have the wisdom to show restraint" (Proverbs 23:4 NIV).

The heavenly Father can use the temptation of workaholism, of never being able to do enough, as an invitation to come to His Son, Jesus, who says, "Come to me all who are weary and heavy burdened and I will give you rest, take My yoke upon you and learn from Me and you shall find rest for your souls" (Matthew 11:28-29 NIV). The heavenly Father is waiting with arms outstretched to embrace you and me and show us the gentle ways of our Older Brother, the Lord Jesus Christ.

The Perfect Parable for the Perfectionist

The voice that says to a man, "you can never do well enough," may be a message that came verbally or non-verbally from his father to him. Most dads communicated this message non-verbally to their sons. Whether said or unsaid, the results are the same in a son's life. Many of us sons never received the heartfelt praise and approval which we longed for. When we become grown men ourselves, we can still hear that voice haunting us. We may look around and see others more financially successful. We may regret that we did not pursue a certain vocational direction when we were younger. We may look at our peers in our vocational field and see them advancing at a faster rate. All of these messages can reinforce the distressing lie that we have believed bit by bit since we were little boys.

After being in business for a time, I joined a Christian mission organization and for five years served as a staff representative to the Marines stationed just a few blocks from where we lived in Kailua, Hawaii.

The time in Hawaii gave me a measure of success and a sense of significance. I felt good about the organization and the career path I was on. Yet Cindy and I believed there were opportunities to develop for me vocationally by moving to the mainland. Cindy and I also believed this would be a good move for the family. But when we arrived in Washington in 1990, I began a "wilderness time" that lasted for about two years when I truly felt that no matter what I did, it just was not good enough. The clarity of my mission was fuzzy and the organization I served with seemed to be in great flux. My ministry "target" was unclear. The identity of the staff was not as defined for me as it had been for me in Hawaii. At this point in my life I felt like a real failure in my area of work and all of my efforts seemed futile and unproductive. I unwisely compared myself to others in my neighborhood who were earning larger salaries and had greater responsibilities in their vocations. They seemed to be more fruitful and those in other professions appeared to have more significance. The perfectionist in me cried out every day; "You are a failure, you don't measure up."

Now, looking back, I can understand why this was all such a struggle for me. I am sure that I unconsciously compared myself at thirty-seven-years of age to my father, who at thirty-seven had already fought in two wars and was on his way to building a national restaurant chain. I had foolishly begun to compare myself with my father and impose pressure upon myself that my heavenly Father never intended for me to carry.

It was in this despair that I began to cry out to God, to my heavenly Father. I could identify with Jonah, who said, "In my distress I called to the LORD, and He answered me. From the depths of the grave I called for help, and You listened to my cry" (Jonah 2:2 NIV),

The heavenly Father's voice spoke most comfortingly to me through a parable found in Matthew, chapter 25. And God used a Bible study of this passage to begin to set me free. What I gleaned from the parable of the talents was that the two servants who were in the end commended by their master were not commended for the quantity of their outward success. One servant was given two talents and gained two more and another servant had five talents and gained five more. The criterion for the master being pleased with them was simply this: *they were faithful to their opportunities.*

Now this may not sound like a life-transforming truth, but for me it was. Like a refreshing breeze, the Holy Spirit was telling me that I was not going to be held responsible for the opportunities that were not given to me but rather for those opportunities that I had been given. I felt liberated. I began to see the foolishness of comparing myself with other "servants," be they my neighbors, co-workers, or my father. All I needed to do was to simply be faithful to what my heavenly Father had given me to do and leave the results up to Him. That gave freedom and joy!

The Call Away from Careerism

For the man caught by the temptation of careerism, who never feels important enough or "famous" enough, the Father also has a gracious provision through His Son. Jesus taught His disciples that a man's greatness is not determined by the quantity of people he controls or influences but rather by the quality of his service toward others that springs from the calm assurance that he is well loved by the Father.

In this world of fierce competition to get the "top dog" position, the man who chooses to be a servant, as his Lord modeled and taught, will amazingly stand in a class by himself. In this world there is always room at the bottom. The Lord Jesus taught by His example that there is dignity in becoming an initiating servant-leader, secure in his position, who humbles himself and meets the needs of other people.

Look at what Jesus said to His disciples in Mark 10 and what he showed them in John 13:3-17. He clearly demonstrated the difference between servanthood and servitude. Jesus knew that He was loved by the Heavenly Father and, based on that, He was secure and motivated to voluntarily serve and meet the needs of His disciples.

Servanthood, as Jesus teaches and models it, is His answer to a father caught up in careerism. Rather than asking himself as he looks at his work where he has the greatest opportunity for power and advancement, this dad can seek to find where he might have the greatest opportunity to serve others, beginning with his own family.

This servant attitude should hold the key for every father when he comes home from work. Rather than looking at his home with a critical eye that probes for the "fly in the ointment" within his kingdom, he should take on the attitude of a willing servant (Philippians 2:3-5). He should ask himself questions such as, "What does my wife need from me right now? What are some ways that I can help meet my kids' needs tonight?" How does a man sustain this attitude through the ups and downs of fatherhood? He can do this simply by continually reminding himself of the heavenly Father's love for him through Christ and following His example in the power of the Holy Spirit.

Moving Away from Materialism

The heavenly Father's provision for a father caught up in the temptation of materialism is learning the attitude of contentment found in His Son. In Matthew 6:25-34, Jesus calls upon His disciples to trust in and be content with the Father's provision. He cautions them not to be distracted by anxiety or overly concerned about the material things of life. The apostle Paul gives essentially the same message when he writes, "But godliness with contentment is great gain. For we brought nothing into the world, and we can take nothing out of it. But if we have food and clothing we will be content with that" (1 Timothy 6:7 NIV).

Contentment is an attitude that is expressed by fathers in a multitude of ways. It can lead a man to decline or delay an opportunity for a promotion that would negatively impact the family at a critical time. Or it may mean living in a smaller, less expensive home where the mortgage is manageable, thereby taking pressure off the family finances. In short, contentment is an attitude with many implications on the decisions a father needs to make. The problem with this whole issue of contentment is that we do have a fixed minimum of our needs but no fixed maximum. The needs that we perceive we have are virually unlimited. One of the ways that we have found helpful for our whole family to grow in contentment is to become involved in short-term missions trips. There is nothing like taking our children to a third-world country for them to gain perspective on what they have and what is "enough."

A Father's Prayer of Transformation

Dear Father,

I praise You for being my perfect provider. You are a God who provides for the birds of the air when they do not reap or store away. You meet their needs, and yet how much more valuable am I to You as Your beloved son (Matthew 6:26,30). I praise you, Father, that every good and perfect gift comes down from Your hand (James 1:17). I praise you that you are the Lord who provides. You have provided for my greatest need, the need for a Saviour through Your Son, Jesus (Romans 5:8). For that I am eternally grateful.

I praise You dear, Father, that when You provide with Your hand You have a loving heart behind the hand, never substituting "presents" for "presence" (Luke 11:11-13). I thank

You for the gift You have given me of physical work and that I have been given the privilege of providing for my family's needs through the work of my hands (Ecclesiastes 5:19-20) partnering with You.

But Father, I confess to You that I have anxiety about being able to meet my family's needs and I worry about You meeting our needs. I know that this doesn't bring honor to You (Matthew 6:31-33).

When I don't see You provide in the way I think You will or should provide, I doubt Your faithful care. Dear Father, I know that my father did the best he could in providing for our family and I thank You for him. But where he fell short, I have carried over to my view of You. Forgive me, Father. And forgive me for any unforgiveness I may still hold toward my father. I will make similar mistakes without Your transforming power at work in me. Like Father, like son. I want to become now like You perfect Father, and I thank You that you have promised to fulfill this desire through Your molding of me to be like Your Son (Romans 8:28-29).

Dear Lord, as I am now seeking to provide for my family, I trust You to provide for us as I do my best to work for You and not as unto men (Colossians 3:23). I come to You Lord Jesus, and join Your work, taking upon myself the yoke that You said gives rest (Matthew 11:28-30). Will You teach us as a family to be restful, grateful and content with Your provision (1 Timothy 6:6-7)? Will You use us to bless others, to be rich in good deeds, generous, and willing to share (1 Timothy 6:18)? Help me to teach my children to be givers in life, not takers (Ephesians 4:28). For You have bought us by Your blood from our own sin to become purified and to be people of Your very own, eager to do what is good (Titus 2:14). In The name of Your Son, Your Perfect Provision, Amen.

Chapter 4

PROTECTING ACTIVELY

"He who fears the Lord has a secure fortress, and for his children it will be a refuge."
(Proverbs 14:26 NIV)

Protection and Distorted Heavenly Father Images

A father who fails to protect his children inadvertently teaches them that the heavenly Father cannot be trusted to protect them as well.

Did you have a father who made you feel safe and secure? Or did he leave you feeling unprotected and vulnerable? There may not be an easy either/or answer to those questions. In some areas you may have felt safe but in other areas of your life you may have felt exposed to danger. When you think of your father as a protector, what comes to your mind? Maybe his hard work kept you safe from the physical elements but his efforts took so much out of him that in so many areas you felt that you had to fend for yourself without his protective hand being there for you.

Do you struggle with watching out for the safety of your children? Maybe you have limited your idea of protector of your children to the mere physical. Dads, if we are not protecting our children we are laying a shaky foundation for them to eventually be able to trust in God's protection. In other words, they will feel insecure in what they have seen (their physical fathers) and will project those insecure feelings towards the One they cannot see, the heavenly Father.

Consider how you were fathered in this area and how you are now fathering as a protector. Think about how your view of the heavenly Father and His protection over your life has been impacted by your family background. And then consider what you are teaching your children right now about God's protective care because of the way that you protect or do not protect them. If you grew up in a home where you felt unprotected you will have a tendency to repeat the same pattern with your family. "Like father, like son" will come true unless you become aware of what needs to change and, through repentance and faith in Christ, take steps to become like Another Father.

Protectors "R" Us!

Being a protector seems just to "ooze" out of us men. We have been given the strength of a warrior's heart. It is revealed in the way we enjoy competition and battle. Watch little boys play. They make sticks into swords and shorter sticks into guns. Adam, our oldest son, used to spend hours in the backyard, much to my gardener wife's chagrin, hacking plants who were "bad guys" with a stick he imagined was a sword. When I was growing up my favorite pre-adolescent pastime was "playing war." My guardian angels worked overtime during my childhood! This eventually led to BB gun fights as I got older. The rule was no shooting above the waist. Yeah, right. Why did we boys do that? My sisters, wife or daughters never even thought about doing those kinds of things. One might say that it was a cultural expectation, but I think a better explanation is that little boys are warriors inside with urges to fight, liberate, and protect.

So how does this built-in desire to be a strong warrior-protector of our family from "bad guys" actually work its way out?

I have been married for over thirty years and I had to use physical force only once to protect my family. I am not particularly proud of this incident but it was one of those times when I felt it was necessary to deal with an abusive man who had become obsessed with my wife. This was before the law provided things such as restraining orders. I prayed, "Lord, please protect me as I go. I ask for forgiveness in advance for what I might do to him." By God's grace and mercy He did protect me and I applied enough force to communicate "the message" to this man in a language he could understand. I do have to admit it did feel kind of good. Protectors "R" us!

We need to look at our protector role in the family as we would see a shock absorber in a car. I used to believe that shock absorbers were kind of a nice accessory for a car to have, a luxury but not a necessity. However, my mechanic told me that my car's shock absorbers are not just something that make for a more comfortable ride but are what keep the wheels of the car on the road. In other words, shock absorbers are vital to a car's safe operation. For a father to exercise his protector role is just that vital to his family's overall safety. Our physical strength is not called upon very often to protect our families, so what do we do with this built-in urge to protect?

Protection from Invisible Enemies

"For our struggle is not against flesh and blood but against the rulers, against the authorities, against the powers of this dark world and against the spiritual forces of evil" (Ephesians 6:12 NIV).

The first area in which a father protects his wife and in his children is in their sense of unique value. Just think of the messages that are coming at your wife and children relentlessly each day through the various media, at school, and in the workplace. The messages they receive day after day all boil down to this: "You are not special, you do not measure up, you are not as talented, pretty, handsome, smart, or popular as others, and therefore you are of less value." These attacks are not on the physical bodies of our family members but upon their very souls. I recently heard about a small town in Georgia that has as its motto, "The town where everybody is somebody." I need to remind my wife and children daily of their incredible value. I must do it often because the attacks upon them are *daily* and they don't let up! When my wife and children come home they need to come to a place "where everybody's somebody" and I am to be the one who sets the pace.

We live in a youth-and-beauty-obsessed society. As your wife gets older it is inevitable that she will gradually lose that youthful external beauty she once had. It is your job to protect her from the lie that her value is attached to a fading youthful physical beauty and thereby declining. You need to be telling her constantly that she is truly beautiful and that you see her *increasing* in the true lasting beauty that does not fade away but only becomes greater in time (1 Peter 3:4).

Jesus provides fathers a powerful picture of Himself as a protector of the sheep. He says, "I tell you the truth, I am the gate for the sheep. All who ever came before me were thieves and robbers, but the sheep did not listen to them" (John 10:7 NIV). Imagine a square corral-like sheep pen with one side a rock wall with a narrow opening where the shepherd would lie down as a "gate" protecting the vulnerable sheep. Dads, we stand at the threshold of our homes protecting our family members in their unique sense of value in much the same way!

Very closely related to this is another aspect of a father's protection. *Every father is responsible for guarding his family from acquiring distorted images of the heavenly Father's character.* The heavenly Father is gracious, merciful, compassionate, and loving. His image and reputation are constantly under attack from our enemy, Satan. He knows that if a person can see the heavenly Father as critical and controlling or as detached and uncaring he will have gone a long way toward keeping whole families in spiritual darkness.

In Jesus' parable of the talents, the factor that determined the difference in behavior of the two faithful servants and the one worthless servant was the view that the worthless servant maintained of the master's character. "I *knew* that you are a hard man, harvesting where you have not sown and gathering where you have not scattered seed. So *I was afraid* and went out and hid your talent in the ground. See, here is what belongs to you" (Matthew 25:24-25 NIV emphasis added).

The man viewed the master who represents the heavenly Father as harsh, unfair, cruel, and oppressive. This produced a fearful insecurity in him and he was unwilling to risk anything because he was so distrustful of the master. He played the hand that he had been dealt way too cautiously. He was playing life so safe that he wound up losing it all. In his case, his eternal destiny was determined by what he mistakenly "knew" to be true about his master's character.

Many men are married to women who received distorted images of the heavenly Father based on the relationship they had with their natural father, stepfather, or father figure. And our children live in a culture that constantly attacks the idea that God is good. He is seen, if it is acknowledged that He in fact exists, either as detached and uninvolved (remember the song by Bette Midler a few years ago, "From A Distance?"), or as one who is stern and angry. When Dad comes home from work what does the family see in his face? Do they see a picture that mirrors the enemy's lies or one that reflects the heavenly Father's true character as revealed through His Son, Jesus Christ? We each have a choice: our lives can *refute* the lies or they can *reinforce* them. Much is at stake, men, as we protect our families from the effects of distorted images of God.

When fathers humbly live out lives that follow Jesus Christ, knowing that they will at times stumble and portray the heavenly Father imperfectly, they will have done well to protect their families from the greatest danger to their eternal destinies, that of developing a distorted image of the heavenly Father. They become the antidotes against perpetuating the disease of carrying around a false image of the heavenly Father that is so rampant in our culture today!

Then third, a father protects the family unity. The biggest attack upon family unity is relational disharmony, or unresolved conflict. A dad needs to be like a finely tuned sensor that makes sure that issues are being resolved and they are not carried over and prolonged over time. And for one very important reason— the Bible says that the devil is looking for a foothold in our lives, and unresolved anger in a family provides just such a foothold (Ephesians 4:26). As fathers we must initiate resolution and reconciliation, always being willing to be "the first to go to the cross," if need be, by admitting any wrong on our part and asking for forgiveness. This is very hard to do. Most men did not see this modeled by their own fathers.

Think of your family members as individual musical instruments who may not be in tune with one other. The best way to get them all tuned together is to tune them all to one tuning fork. The result is that they will automatically be in tune with each other. Dads, our role is to sound out the melody of Father's heart in our homes. He is the ultimate "tuning fork" who will produce family unity and harmony. Of course our first job is to make sure that we, ourselves, are first tuned to Him in repentance and faith constantly re-aligning our lives to His truth.

Another attack upon family unity is activity overload. This is very subtle but can be deadly. It may take the form of an increased number of nights out or the doing of lots of "good things" as individuals that pull us away from family togetherness. These threats can appear as innocent as taking on extra sports commitments that gradually grow. Dad, you need to sit down regularly with your wife and discuss the pace of the family's life. Most families are moving way too fast today. A place to start in slowing down the family is to plan family mealtimes. Guard the family dinner hour if at all possible!

Then still another attack upon the unity of the family comes from the explosion of family-divisive technology. I am not even talking here about the *content* of the messages received from the technology. Just look at what television, the personal computer, computer games, and cell phones are doing to the family's sense of unity. They are breaking up our lives into little compartments, isolating us from each other while simultaneously connecting us and our children more strongly to the outer world.

Think about the fact that for hundreds of years, when a family was cold they huddled together around the fireplace. When they were hot they sat on the front porch and sipped lemonade. With the advent of indoor heating and air conditioning, it is no longer necessary for families to congregate together. Because it is no longer necessary in the physical sense it does not mean it is not still necessary in the emotional and spiritual sense.

Technology can be either our servant or our master. In many families today it is the master and controller of the home. It is the exercising of a father's protector role that will prevent technology from enslaving his family. Dads, if we do not stand in the way of this technological invasion of our homes, who will?

Another place where fathers protect their families is in the area of their children's own sin and foolishness. Families today are being inundated with immoral messages through television, radio, film, and the internet. Fathers are called to stand in the way and protect. Have you limited your idea of a protector of your children to the mere physical, overlooking the moral? King Solomon wrote to his son in the book of Proverbs with an emphasis upon warning his son of the many moral pitfalls awaiting him in life. Some of these dangers include immorality (2:18, Chapters 5-7), laziness (20:4), get-rich-quick schemes (12:11), negative peer pressure (13:20), impulsiveness (15:22, 20:18), gossip (16:28), and anger (16:32), just to name a few.

How Fathers Go AWOL

If a father's protection provides such a key to his family's safety, why do so many of us fathers allow ourselves to get pulled away from this crucial role so easily?

As I have reflected on this I can see that Satan's strategy is to pervert the very warrior-protector spirit that is built into us men and thus in some way render us ineffective in protecting our homes. *The most obvious perversion is to use our strength to control and even abuse family members.* Such a father becomes unsafe, an attacker himself within his own home. These abusers are often hard to detect from the outside. But behind closed doors they are angry, controlling men, seeking to impose their will upon the family by sheer force of will. The warrior is no longer protecting his family but rather seeking to dominate them. The fox is now guarding the hen house! Sadly, this tragedy is taking place in far too many homes across America and, even more sadly, in homes of faith.

Another way that fathers leave their post is to take their focus off their home and put it on the pursuit of conquest of other "lands," gravitating to places where they imagine that they will be more appreciated and rewarded, thereby leaving their home vulnerable to attack. This is a story being written over and over again in families today. As discussed in the previous chapter, when a man gives his best energy to the workplace he can have nothing but emotional leftovers to offer his family. Then he has done what Jesus warned His disciples about when He asked, "What good will it be for a man if he gains the whole world, yet forfeits his soul?" (Matthew 16:25 NIV).

Proverbs 17:8 (NIV) states, "Like a bird that strays from its nest is a man who strays from his home." This reflects a very interesting thing about how eagles protect their young. The mother and father eagle both go out and hunt prey to bring fresh meat for their eaglets. But their little eaglets have an enemy. Snakes will slither up to the nest from below and devour them. The little eaglets know instinctively to screech if they see something moving around them that is not another eagle. If the parent eagle strays too far from the nest to hunt for food, he may not hear the screech or see the snake. Once the snake is spotted one of the parents will go right after it and often take it in its talons and drop it on a rock below to crush it. What a picture for fathers. Just as these eagles, we fathers will be futile providers for the nest if we stray too far and forget our priority to first *protect* our children.

A straying father's work no longer provides family needs but becomes an issue of either meeting insatiable ego needs or a desire to please others. The affirmation and rewards, whether they be in the workplace, church, or the community, can be awfully tempting to seek outside the home. The warrior may admirably conquer but he has failed to protect. What a tragedy!

A third way that we fathers lose our protective influence over our families is by seeking to escape the pressure of being the protector. Let's admit it, protecting is a weighty responsibility and it is a pressure that can feel unbearable at times. To live out their warrior yearnings and at the same time escape the pressure, many fathers will escape into excessive recreation or pursuit of entertainment that distracts from their primary role. That is not to say that there is something wrong with going to a ball game or watching television occasionally. Nor is it wrong to play a round of golf once in awhile. But the question is always this, "How much do I think about my responsibilities when I am not doing them"? "How upset do I get when my team loses?" "How upset do I get when I do poorly in this recreational pursuit?" If we find that too much energy is being expended there, it is a good indication that this pressure release has now become a controlling obsession in our lives, distracting attention and draining protective energy away from our families.

A Father's Prayer of Transformation

Dear Father,

I Praise You for being my secure fortress and a fortress for my children You are my refuge (Proverbs 14:26). I praise You that You hold over my life a "Father-Filter" and that nothing can ever come into my life that has not first passed through that filter. You have wisely determined that in Your strength I can stand up to any test or temptation that You allow and You provide the way of escape (1 Corinthians 10:13). I thank You that though I have been hurt I can never be truly harmed by anyone else's sin against me. I thank You that You have promised to work all things together for my good, for my transformation to be like Your Son. You will work in everything that comes into my life as I trust Your good purpose for me (Romans 8:28-29).

Father, as I approach your awesome throne with my advocate, the Lord and Savior Jesus Christ at my side (1 John 2:1-2) I come boldly and confidently because of Him and who You have made me in Him (Ephesians 3:12). I come to You admitting that I have doubts about Your protection of me. As I think back at my childhood through my adulthood years, I can see that it appeared that I was left vulnerable to forces that were aimed at my destruction.

These experiences have made it hard for me to trust in Your protection. In my head I know Father, that You are my Protector but it is hard to trust You in my heart. Lord, as that one father said to Your Son, Jesus, "Lord, I believe; help my unbelief" (Mark 9:24). Will You now help me grasp Your protective love in my innermost being? And now as a father myself, I confess that I have left my children vulnerable and unprotected in many areas they have needed my protection. Like father, like son. But Lord, in Your transforming power for those who look to You (2 Corinthians 3:16-18) I call upon You to make me the protector of my children that they need me to be. Beyond that I ask that You protect them in areas where I cannot be there for them—in the realm of the spirit. I am aware, Father, that our battle is not against flesh and blood but against the spiritual forces of evil in the heavenly places (Ephesians 6:12).

Dear Father, I know that You love my wife and my children infinitely more than I love them myself and You know what is truly, eternally best for them. I pray that You will put a hedge of protection (Job 1:10) around each of my family members. Father put within them a deep sense of security, of Your protection, of Your hand upon their lives so that their faith in You will be fully in You and will not be shaken no matter what comes their way (1 Corinthians 2:6). I know that Satan wants to sift them away from You like wheat, but I pray that their faith in You will not fail, and as they pass their tests that they will be able to strengthen others (Luke 23:31-32). Father, whatever suffering that You wisely allow into their lives would You please use it to prepare them to be vessels of your fatherly compassion and comfort to others who also suffer (2 Corinthians 1:3-4)?

And Father, God of all grace, who has called me and my family to Your eternal glory, after we have suffered a little while, I trust you to restore us and make us strong, firm and steadfast. To You, Father, be the power forever and ever (1 Peter 3:10-11). In The name of Jesus who is my Protector, Amen.

Chapter 5

DISCIPLINING APPROPRIATELY

"He who spares the rod hates his son, but he who loves him is careful to discipline him."
(Proverbs 13:24 NIV)

Discipline And Distorted Heavenly Father Images

A father can distort the picture of God's holiness or His compassion either by being overly oppressive or overly permissive in the discipline of his children.

The oppressive father teaches his children that the heavenly Father is harsh and arbitrary in his discipline of his children. Children with this kind of father will have a tendency to struggle with resting in God's love. All that they read about God's love may be understood intellectually but will not be embraced emotionally. They will feel that God is that "cosmic killjoy" ready to pounce upon their every fault.

But on the other hand, the permissive father teaches his children that the heavenly Father is soft on sin and they will tend to have a hard time having a reverent attitude toward God. The children of a permissive dad will tend to see God as a lovable softy. They will lack the fear of the Lord that is so essential for them to gain a life of wisdom (Proverbs 1:7). As the theologian John Piper has said, "Beware of the fruit of love separated from the root of truth." The father who showers his children with affection but does not put limits on their behavior does them no favors.

When you consider how you were disciplined, which extreme did your father seem to fall into? Some fathers vacillated between the two extremes—oppressive and harsh when they did discipline but permissive and neglectful the rest of the time. That experience may still be coloring your view of God, the heavenly Father. Is your discipline of your children teaching them about a God who is both holy and is serious about sin and who is also compassionate and loving in dealing with his children? It takes His gracious involvement to paint that balanced picture.

Today, in 21st century North America, the permissive father generally presents a greater threat than the oppressive father. A plant can be destroyed by either stomping on it or by neglecting it to death. I believe neglect of paternal discipline poses the greatest danger to families today.

A few years ago I came across a book that captures the dilemma facing parents today when it comes to discipline. It is a book like none I had read before. The title says it all, *Spoiled Rotten*, by Fred Gosman.

"The question isn't what's good for the family, but what's good for Julie. In millions of American homes, children are in control, receiving the same kind of fawning and deferential treatment formerly reserved for elderly parents who might have lived with us.

We actually *consult* with our kids as if they were equals. If we want to go to grandma's and they don't, we waste our time explaining reasons for the visit. Why not just order them to the car? Or, if Joey doesn't want to wear a new sweater from his aunt, we negotiate, hoping he'll not cause a family scene by refusing to wear it. Why do we dignify our kids with reasoning powers beyond their years?

Does all our catering seem to be working? Weren't the little ones more stable when they were seen and not heard? When parents didn't have to watch them play? When they weren't treated like equals? When we decided which TV show the family watched?

Children who have been treated like the center of the universe can't get along with other children or, worse, sometimes even themselves. And disciplining them is a difficult challenge indeed."

Then Gosman continues.

"In one of the Beach Boys' famous songs, a female motorist has 'fun, fun, fun, 'til her daddy takes the T-Bird away.'

If we were to update that song to reflect discipline today, the girl would still be driving, cruising the freeway without a care in the world. Her father still opposes her behavior, but instead of taking away the car, he keeps giving her ineffective warnings. For the old man isn't tough enough to maintain the standards he claims to hold. He'd rather be liked by his daughter and pray for her safety than do what's right.

We have a society of second, third, and even fourth chances. Children can misbehave with impunity, knowing that initial deviations will be met with barely raised eyebrows rather than swift consequences. We've become paralyzed at the prospect of holding our kids accountable for their actions, regardless of how clearly we enunciate our standards."

And a couple more paragraphs really drive this point in…

"We threaten and threaten, but never enforce discipline. We believe we're giving 'second chances,' but that's not true. Perhaps a hundred times in their lives, maybe thousands, these children have received, "second chances" from people more interested in being liked than in helping. If all the previous threats didn't work, why do we go on naïvely thinking the next one will?

Why do so many of us need to be liked? It just doesn't come with the territory. If we want to be liked, we should give out dollars on street corners, but we shouldn't expect to have a friendship with our kids. It's like vinegar and oil, night and day. The minute we care unreasonably if our children like us, we are theirs."[1]

Do Gosman's comments resonate with you? They do with me! Our culture has forgotten the proper role of the father as a disciplinarian. We have become so afraid of being termed "abusive" or "authoritarian" that we have swung the pendulum to the opposite extreme and have tried to just be our kids' friends. Friendship with our children is a worthy goal to achieve as they become adults, but that is not the appropriate relationship to have with them while they are growing up in our home.

It was a hot August afternoon and my first experience as a head coach for a five-year-old boys' soccer team. I found myself inundated with perhaps a dozen wild five-year-old boys. We aptly named the team "The Stallions." As I was standing in the shade discussing expectations with my team, along came a boy who had just lost his father in a tragic climbing accident on Mount Rainier. This little boy felt the sympathy of all of us. And I so much wanted to be able to help him and be a type of "father figure" as his soccer coach. But my efforts felt so futile. I can vividly remember how I called to him as he took the ball, kicked it out of bounds, and just kept kicking until he was far off the field.

This boy's dear mother was not able to control him and I could see that even at that age he was undisciplined. I am sure the tragedy made discipline even a greater challenge as this mother sought to nurture her two young sons after her tragic loss. We lost touch with this boy until recently when we heard that, as an adolescent, he had been caught breaking into homes in the neighborhood stealing underwear from women's bedrooms. Now he is doing things more serious than kicking the soccer ball out of bounds and not listening to his coach. He is breaking the law. I have no doubt that he needed lots of compassion during that time after he lost his father but what he also needed was a strong, firm disciplinarian in his life, which apparently he did not receive. I have known situations where children rebel and they have had a loving, disciplining father so I am not implying that it is only the fault of a lack of a disciplining father that causes this type of rebellion. But it clearly it is a factor.

This boy's lack of discipline is not an isolated incident. It matches what Gosman said in his book and what many of us can attest to when we observe children today. But how did we get into this mess? There are many ways to look at the dilemma we find ourselves in but let's start by examining a few broad social trends that prevailed during the last half of the 20th century.

The Cultural Quicksand

During the 1950s, American parents emerged from the twin shadows of the Great Depression and World War II determined to give their children the life that they had been denied. The children who grew up during that time, "Baby Boomers," were overly indulged. Parents became centered upon them. Dr. Benjamin Spock, the parenting guru of the time, directed parents not to spank their children. In the 1960s the Boomers were coming of age and they were taught to question all authority. Unfortunately, from the Civil Rights movement, the war in Vietnam, and the Watergate cover-up, much authority proved to be quite unworthy of trust.

The 1970s became known as the "Me Decade," with every special interest group demanding its own rights. Women won the right to choose abortion on demand, married couples won the right for no-fault divorce, and darkness continued to descend over the family. Television at that time mirrored and promoted this evil by increasingly portraying fathers as pathetic characters. By the1990s there was a further change. Fathers went from being the wise patriarchs of *Bonanza, Ozzie and Harriet* and *Father Knows Best*, to the hapless buffoons found on *Married With Children* and *The Simpsons*.

It is pretty easy to see this cultural slide from the strong disciplining father to the pathetic picture of today. But how does that happen to individual fathers? What keeps fathers from playing an active disciplinarian role in their children's lives? What makes it so difficult for fathers to buck this cultural tide and write a different script for their own fathering?

WHY MANY FATHERS DO NOT DISCIPLINE TODAY

A Lack of Positive Modeling

Perhaps the biggest reason that a father falls down as a disciplinarian is poor modeling from his father. Like father, like son. His father may have been absent through simple inattention, an over commitment to his job, or a lack of commitment to his role due to a cohabitation relationship or through divorce.. Many fathers today were raised by men who just wanted to be their buddy and didn't want to "play the heavy." Or their dad may have experienced a childhood at the other end of the spectrum of discipline extremes that was filled with abuse, anger, sarcasm, put-downs, and shame. Either extreme makes it hard for a father to understand what healthy discipline looks like.

A father will either repeat his father's abusive failures or run so far from them that he falls into passivity. Either way, this poor modeling sets him up to fail as a disciplinarian unless he seeks some outside help.

A Lack of Self-discipline

Before a man can hope to discipline his children he must first discipline himself. He must have the self-control to follow through and do the hard things when he needs to. He needs to be able to say "No" to instant gratification and choose to do what will produce the greatest lasting benefit.

To discipline your children tests your commitment to follow through. You will be faced with the reality that you need to provide a consequence for your children's misbehavior and you need to do it even when it is inconvenient, which it nearly always is. The self-discipline issue is why so many fathers fall flat on their face right out of the fathering gate. As that song of the early 70s, "Sunshine," by Jonathan Edwards, said, "He can't even run his own life, I'll be d——d if he'll run mine." Many fathers may be disciplined in other areas such as their work, but when it comes to disciplining their children they would rather follow the path of least resistance.

Over the years Cindy and I have owned a number of dogs. There is a time during the puppy stage when we enroll our dog in obedience school. In one class the dog trainer told us all something I will never forget: "If you treat your dog like a human, he will treat you like a dog." We all laughed a nervous laugh knowing that our little canine friends had already gained "top-dog status" around our homes. How could we let these cute furry little mammals rule over us? Because it was simply easier in the short run not to have to confront their canine wills. We tended to follow the path of least resistance.

The path of least resistance in parenting is not to confront, not to correct, not to deal with a child's sinful, willful rebellion. This is the wide road that seems like the right road, but it leads to destruction (Proverbs 14:12), Children will, just like those dogs, become the ones in charge in their homes when parents abdicate their right to set and enforce the rules. Sure, in the short run it is easier. Just as it is easier to not exercise, to not turn off the television or the computer, to not push the plate away, to not pull the weeds growing in the yard. In the short run, yes, inaction is always easier, but there will always come a day of reckoning.

A House Divided Cannot...Discipline

A current cause of many fathers' failure in discipline is related to the challenges caused through divorce or by situations where the father never married his children's mother in the first place. Since the 1970s, our culture has been increasingly cursed with the scourge of divorce to the point that today roughly one out of every two marriages fails. When a marriage bond is never formed, as in the case of cohabitation, or is destroyed by divorce, a powerful disciplinarian team is rendered much less effective. This is especially true when a state of hostility continues to exist between the mother and father. The children are caught in the middle and they often learn to manipulate the situation to their (temporary) advantage. Generally, in our society, the mother is given custody of the children and the father is left with visitation rights. In this situation it is especially difficult for the father to play his disciplinarian role with any effectiveness or consistency.

When a dad does not have the backing of his children's mother the children will tend to mirror the disrespect that the mother expresses to her children about their father. Also, a child who is manipulative and who does not want to live under a father's discipline, can accuse that father of being abusive in discipline.

These accusations will be taken seriously by a distrustful spouse and a court system justifiably designed to protect children.

Simple Unbelief in What God Says about Human Nature

A fourth reason that fathers today do not discipline their children is unbelief in what God says about human nature when left to itself. The Bible gives clear warnings to parents about the dangers of not training or disciplining their children. For one reason or another many fathers refuse to believe what the Bible portrays as reality. The Bible warns that if a child grows up to disrespect his parents he will face a tragic future.

"The eye that mocks a father, that scorns obedience to a mother will be pecked out by ravens of the valley, will be eaten by vultures" (Proverbs 30:17 NIV).

"Folly is bound up in the heart of a child, but the rod of discipline will drive it far from him" (Proverbs 22:15 NIV).

A father who does not discipline does not simply believe what the Bible says about his child's heart, that it is "deceitful above all things and beyond cure" (Jeremiah 17:9 NIV). He does not see that his job is to "train (his) child in the way he should go and when he is old, he will not turn from it" (Proverbs 22:6 NIV).

The book of Proverbs can best be understood as probabilities or "truisms" rather than promises. This is wisdom literature, though fully inspired by the Spirit of God-it makes allowance for the exception to the rule and the freedom of the human will. Essentially what Solomon says to parents is that if you do the training of your children on the front end of their lives they will benefit throughout their adulthood, just like those puppies in obedience school.

But many fathers do not believe this. They may believe that children are basically good and it is their environment, other people crossing their will, obstructing their potential, who pose the greatest danger. They may foolishly see their primary role as one who provides the best athletic coaching, academic opportunities, or whatever else they think their children need to bolster their self-esteem.

The Fear Factor

The fifth reason that I have observed as to why many fathers do not discipline their children today is that they are simply afraid to do it. No doubt fear is big factor. This fear can be divided into two basic categories: the fear of failure and the fear of rejection.

The fear of failure - A man can only "fail" in his own eyes if he invests himself to succeed in a certain arena. He needs to gets into the game to ever risk failing in the game. Psychologist William James wisely observed about human nature that a person's self-esteem depends entirely upon what he or she backs himself to do or be. When a man does not make the effort he can protect himself from the experience of failure. This has many applications for men who have been wounded by their own father's family failures.

A man who watched his parents fail in their marriage may choose to avoid getting married so as not to risk the failure of divorce. A man may choose to always play it safe in his career and thus protect himself from the possibility of failure. The couch potato can feel better about himself than a second-place Olympic athlete or a starting NFL quarterback after the loss of a playoff game because he did not invest himself in the contest. This is indeed a strange phenomenon.

In the same way, if a father does not invest himself in the discipline process he can fool himself into believing that he is not a failure since he never made the attempt. This is a temptation for the man who experienced overcorrection from his father. He operates in fear of repeating the same things with his children that his father did with him.

The fear of rejection – In the Bible we learn about Eli, Israel's high priest who failed miserably as a father. Fear seems to have been at work in Eli when he failed to discipline his two sons. God spoke to him, "Why do you honor your sons more than Me by fattening yourselves on the choice parts of every offering made by the people of Israel?" (I Samuel 2:29 NIV). Later we read that Eli was very much aware of what his sons were doing in their gluttonous oppression of the people who came to worship and their sexual exploitation of the women who worked at the entrance of the tent of meeting. Eli's sin, for which God judged his family, was that his sons God and Eli failed to restrain them (I Samuel 3:13).

A father can fear his own children's rejection of him. This happens especially if he and his wife are not lovingly united in their discipline effort as a team. If a husband and wife have not come to agreement as to how they will discipline, then this can be a subject that many husbands find easier to avoid all together. Imposing discipline can bring a man into conflict with his wife.

The Husband-Wife Team Is Ideal

"God blessed *them* and said to *them*, "Be fruitful and increase in number, fill the earth and subdue (rule over) it" (Genesis 1:28 NIV emphasis added). It was God's plan that a husband and wife team form a special partnership and rule together. This is one of the reasons that divorce or domestic violence that causes a break in this bond is so devastating to the upbringing of godly children. "Has not the LORD made them one? In flesh and spirit they are His. And why one? Because he was seeking godly offspring. God tells us to guard ourselves in our spirit and not to break with the wife of our youth. 'I hate divorce,' says the LORD God of Israel, 'and I hate a man covering himself with violence as well as with his garment,' says the LORD God Almighty" (Malachi 2:15-16 NIV).

Let's not overlook the obvious here. A father's size and strength can come in handy, especially as the children get older. A young son should never have any doubt that if he challenges his mother's authority he will then have to contend with his father as well. This could be called the proper "fear factor." Now, of course, if a child is trained to respect his mother when he is young there should never be a physical challenge of her authority as the child grows into young adulthood.

What A Dad Contributes To The Discipline Team

Objectivity And A Justice Perspective

God has made men different than women, and I am not talking here about just the obvious physical differences. The following generalizations about men and women do not always fit neatly, but in parenting men have certain tendencies, even as do women. Generally, men have a keener sensor towards objective truth with their children and women tend to excel in showing compassion. A father brings a sense of justice, fairness, and duty into the normal parenting equation and a mother brings grace and sympathy in the midst of disobedience. One man and one woman, both made in the image of God, together provide a more balanced picture of God than either one does separately.

Neither gender is right or wrong. Both bring needed perspectives. The man needs to remind the woman of the task at hand and the woman needs to remind him of the importance of maintaining the interpersonal relationships. Sometimes Cindy and I don't follow this general male/female pattern, but this appreciation of differences still works for us because we come at parenting from complementary perspectives. Over time we have learned to listen to each other and incorporate both justice and mercy in our discipline.

Dad Motivates Toward Change Differently Than Mom

When you read the apostle Paul's first letter to the Thessalonians you can see how he compares his care for these people to both a mother's and a father's love. Notice how he explains his motherly care. "We were gentle among you like a mother caring for her little children" (1 Thessalonians 2:7 NIV). Now note the difference as he describes his fatherly love, "For you know that we dealt with each of you as a father deals with his own children, encouraging, comforting and urging you live lives worthy of God, who calls you into his kingdom and glory" (1 Thessalonians 2:11 NIV). The difference is not *contradictory*, but *complementary* care. A father calls out his children to become all they were created to be, while their mother provides the unconditional acceptance that they also greatly need.

Think back to your own childhood. Who did you want most to be proud of you, your mother or your father? For most men, their mother was a "given." But for their father to be proud of them, now that meant something. As sons they longed to hear their affirmation and they were ready to respond to his challenges. Their father could motivate them to do things that their mother could not, not only because of the "fear factor" but also because of their special God-infused longing to make that particular man, their father, proud of them.

No matter how disappointing the relationship, children may have had with their father, there still lies within them an innate desire to please him, and that is a huge "carrot" that can benefit a father in his discipline of his children.

Special Power Lies in a Father's Example

Again the apostle Paul gives us a picture of fathering through his use of a fathering metaphor to teach a spiritual truth to the Corinthian believers. He came to them as a disciplining spiritual father. Because of his spiritual authority he had influence that was unique. But what gave power to his authority is that he was living his life as an example to them so he could say "do as I say *and* as I do." Even though they had gone off course in several areas, he says,

"I am not writing this to shame you, but to warn you as my dear children. Even though you have ten thousand guardians in Christ, you do not have many fathers, for in Christ Jesus I became your father through the gospel. Therefore *I urge you to imitate me*" (1 Corinthians 4:14-15 NIV emphasis added).

A father's model is foundational to his influence upon his children. I recall a dark period in my childhood when I was thirteen years old. I felt as if my life was over. I was barely passing my classes. Where I had been successful in sports previously, I now felt like a failure. I became a loner at school where before I had a number of friends. I began to use drugs to numb the pain and loneliness. Even the one time that my parents caught me I only felt their wrath and anger. I felt so lost and alone.

Then that summer our family moved to Hawaii. My father was building the house that both he and my mother had long dreamed of, overlooking beautiful Kaneohe Bay, Hawaii. My dad gave me the opportunity to work on the house. This amounted to such glamorous jobs as digging ditches and picking at basalt rocks, but it was like a fresh start, a new lease on life.

That summer gave me a taste of succeeding at something and I began to feel good about myself again. What I drew from that experience was based on my father's example. I saw him model hard work, and though I had very little work experience before that summer, I was able to do what I saw my father do.

When we speak of discipline, there is probably no other component of a father's role in his children's lives that has as much impact upon their spiritual receptivity. It is discipline that in a special way prepares children's hearts for a relationship with their heavenly Father.

WHY GODLY DISCIPLINE HAS RAMIFICATIONS FOR THE LIFE TO COME

Principle #1-Horizontal (Human) Bitterness Causes Vertical (God) Blindness

This principle works mightily in the father-child relationship. Imagine a man who still carries unresolved anger toward his father. He has not forgiven his father and now he is a father himself. His children, through their own sinfulness, will eventually tug on that anger chord in their father, and the bitterness and the anger will spew out upon them like volcanic lava. The children's "unfairness sensor" will be activated and they in turn will hold a grudge against their father. Like father, like son (and daughter). Sin that has not been confessed or forgiven continues to fester and grow with each succeeding generation, moving down the family line like the proverbial snowball growing as it rolls down the hill.

This bitterness can prevent a child from "seeing" the Lord and personally encountering Him. The writer of the book of Hebrews says it this way, "Make every effort to live in peace with all men and be holy; without holiness no one will see the Lord. See to it that no one misses the grace of God and that no bitter root grows up to cause trouble and defile man" (Hebrews 12:14-15 NIV).

It never ceases to amaze me that when I have the opportunity to speak to a group of men and I ask them, "How many of you can remember a time when your father came to you and asked for forgiveness?" The percentage is usually somewhere between zero and ten percent. Tragic!

The Apostle Paul warned fathers, "Fathers, do not embitter your children or they will become discouraged" (Colossians 3:21 NIV). A father embitters or causes bitterness in his children when he holds them to a high standard but does not live up to it himself. And worse yet, he does not humbly admit when he fails, nor does he ask for forgiveness. This is what defiles and spiritually blinds many children to the reality of a merciful, compassionate heavenly Father.

All of this relates directly to your father role. Since the first person a father must discipline is *himself*, part of that discipline is living a life in which he is willing to be accountable to others, even to his own children. When you sin against your children in some way, this is an excellent opportunity to teach them that you have placed yourself under the same authority that you are expecting them to live under. You also teach them that all people need to admit wrong and ask for forgiveness—even dads and moms. This encourages them to see that when they do wrong they can do the same thing. If you model a prideful spirit and denial of wrong to your children then they will be blinded to the light of both God's holiness and His forgiveness through Christ. "But if anyone causes one of these little ones who believe in Me to sin it would be better for him to have a large millstone hung around his neck and to be drowned in the depths of the sea" (Matthew 18:6 NIV).

Principle # 2 Horizontal (Human) Bonding Can Cause Vertical (God) Blindness

If a father is more bonded to and more committed to his own children than to God he will create dangerous spiritual conditions for them.

This is exactly what happened with Eli and his two sons as described earlier. He was more concerned with not upsetting his boys than with pleasing God. So he did not confront them with their sin (I Samuel 2:29, 3:13). And David, "a man after God's own heart," allowed his love for his son Adonijah to blind him from his need to honor the Lord first in faithfully disciplining his son. Speaking of Adonijah, who illegitimately sought to exalt himself as king, we read, "His father had never interfered with him by asking 'Why do you behave as you do?' He was very handsome and was born next after Absalom" (1 Kings 1:6 NIV).

A father who neglects to confront his children will lead them into spiritual blindness. Such children will grow up to become wise in their own estimation of themselves, blinded to their dark side. In Proverbs, a wise man named Agur writes, "There are those who curse their father and do not bless their mother, who are pure in their own eyes, and yet are not cleansed of their own filth" (Proverbs 30:11-12 NIV).

If children grow up without restraints, boundaries, or discipline they will grow up self-deceived, "pure in their own eyes," with no sense of their need for a Saviour. This blinds these children to their need for the cross of Christ. Could our excessive concern with protecting our children's self-esteem today play right into the devil's hands by causing our children to feel good about themselves-even in their sinful rebellion?

A self-centered, disobedient, and unrepentant child is unprepared to meet the Lord. "This is the verdict: Light has come into the world, but men loved darkness instead of light because their deeds were evil. Everyone who does evil hates the light and will not come into the light for fear that his deeds will be exposed" (John 3:19-20 NIV).

There is much at stake spiritually for your children if you fail to discipline in a godly way. You can either pass on bitterness and unforgiveness to your children through harshness or you can passively fail to confront or cross your children's wills. Either way produces spiritual blindness in your children.

The great news is that godly discipline is attainable for regular dads. It comes with the help and guidance of the heavenly Father who wishes to walk alongside each of His beloved sons through His indwelling Spirit.

Biblical Guidelines for Effective Discipline

1. **Be settled in your mind that it is for their good.** This may sound simple, but many fathers are not convinced. Sure there are many other motives that can be at work such as getting peace and quiet in the home or even taking their frustration out on one who is weaker. But at its very core, firm and loving discipline is for the good of children (Hebrews 12:10-11). This really comes down to what you truly believe. If you believe in either of the two lies that your child is either a blank slate or that he is inherently good, then you will not be wholehearted in loving discipline. You will doubt that you are really doing the right and loving thing. Get it settled in your mind once and for all that discipline is for your child's good.

2. **Don't threaten and repeat.** Don't threaten and repeat! Don't threaten and repeat!" The anger of man does not bring about the righteous life that God desires" (James 1:19 NIV). When you threaten and repeat those threats until you get obedience, you are actually training your children to wait "until you really mean it." It also puts you in the situation where you do not actually follow through until you become angry. This is a lose-lose situation. Full disclosure here: I have fallen into this trap many times. I have had to work on explaining the expectation and the consequences if that is not met, and then, in a matter of fact manner, following through with the consequences.

3. **Catch your kids doing something right.** This is an old John Wooden coaching principle that is so important in parenting. It is so easy in the area of discipline to dwell so much on the negative that you miss the opportunities to praise your kids when they really do well in the things you expect. When a father gets too busy he often misses the opportunities to reinforce positive behavior by words of appreciation and recognition of positive efforts. Let's say I am working on training my children to speak respectfully to me and to each other. If I notice my two sons getting along well, I will put my arms around them and tell them that I am proud of the way they are treating each other. It takes me ten seconds but it pays off. If my youngest daughter listens to me and doesn't try to finish my sentences for me, I will make a point to tell her I notice that she is respectfully listening to me, again reinforcing something positive. By doing this, it

increases our positive interaction and makes the time when I need to talk about something negative more bearable for them—and for me.

4. **Know the difference between "foolishness" and "childishness."** Foolishness occurs when children rebel and challenge their parents' authority. Childishness is when they just make an immature mistake or don't act their age. Here's a test you can use: if your child accidentally spills a glass of milk, that's childishness. But if that same child takes that same milk and pours it on his brother's head in anger, now that's foolishness and that needs correction. The child knows that it is not right to hurt or humiliate his brother and that he has disobeyed his parents.

5. **Respect your child's dignity.** A couple of things come to mind here. The first thing that Cindy and I have found helpful as a good rule of thumb is to praise publicly and reprove privately. For a child to receive a spanking is a humbling thing and it should be done privately, but to receive a compliment in front of others is greatly appreciated. Another is the idea of talking with our kids about issues "outside of conflict," that is not in the heat of the battle when our emotions are high and their defenses are up. We will carefully pick an appropriate time and then talk about the issue using the "Oreo approach." We start with affirmation, deal with the issue and then end with affirmation. Like the Oreo cookie, it is much more palatable for them to receive negative comments when it is surrounded by the chocolate wafers of affirmation.

6. **Don't overload them with too many things to work on at once.** When the heavenly Father disciplines us, He generally puts His finger on one thing at a time. Let's say there are three or four things that are concerning you about one of your kids. It is important to discuss with your wife what one thing should be focused on, what is the priority. This could mean holding a little family meeting and discussing the issue. The problem behavior could be explained, the appropriate consequences if the behavior continues, and you could end with something affirming like, "I know you don't want to act like this" and "you are better than this."

7. **Whenever possible warn of the consequences ahead of time.** Our family has a tradition of going to Cannon Beach Christian Conference Center in Oregon every summer. Last summer we thought it was time that we let our kids stay in their own rooms and allow them some extra freedoms. But then we made clear to them that if they did not go to their youth group meetings they would be staying back with us in our room (a fate worse than death for a teen). Needless to say they behaved because they knew that it was a privilege conditioned upon their keeping their side of the bargain.

8. **Make the consequences fit the child and do not remove the natural consequences.**
It is important for you to know what experiences each of your children will perceive as negative consequences. There is a time to phase out spanking. Spanking is appropriate for young children but is decreasingly effective as they get older. Cindy and I have used consequences such as isolation, removal of privileges, and restrictions. By the time our kids started school we were about ninety-percent done with using corporal punishment in our discipline. Yet each child is so different. For one of our younger sons, to be confined to his room for two hours is like doing hard time at Leavenworth Prison. But our older son, guitar in hand, would welcome the solitude; it would be a reward. There are situations where our children must face the natural consequences of their actions and we should not be so quick to shield them from them. For example, if they are careless with somebody's property it is helpful for them to do something to pay the person back. That is a natural consequence. They really do not need additional punishment on top of that.

9. **View the discipline process as a gradual opening of a box.** One of the concepts that Cindy and I have built our parenting around has been the idea of providing each of our children with a gradually expanding box. We explain this concept often with the kids like this: the walls of the box represent their boundaries. When they were young the box was small. As they grew and demonstrated that they could be trusted with responsibility, the walls of the box expanded outward giving them more freedom. If they acted irresponsibly or in an untrustworthy manner, the walls didn't expand or they would contract a bit. The message is that it is up to them how much freedom they will be given while in our home. The goal is that when they leave home as young adults the box walls are flattened out and they are self-disciplined. It is much easier to open your children's box slowly than to panic when they reach their teen years and try to force them back into small box. That is a sure-fire recipe for rebellion.

10. **Regularly discuss your children's attitudes and behavior with their mother.** Your wife, your children's mother, is your greatest fathering asset. She has insights that you do not have. Most likely she spends the greatest amount of time with your children. But she also needs your input and perspective. She may sometimes be too close to the situation to have a clear perspective. I have found with Cindy and me, especially with our sons, that she is able to address my blind spots. At times I get my own issues tangled up with theirs. Yet at the same time I have some insights about them that she doesn't have because I understand firsthand, by personal experience, what a boy needs.

Some Final Words

To discipline a child is a high calling. It can also be a lonely job at times. If you are serious about this you will at times be misunderstood, under-appreciated and wrongly accused. But being obedient in this challenging area will draw you into the loving arms of Jesus and enable you to enjoy the heavenly Father's love and good pleasure in a new dimension.

"Whoever has my commands and obeys them, he is the one who loves me. He who loves me will be loved by my Father, and I too will love him and show myself to him" (John 14:21 NIV).

A Father's Prayer Of Transformation

Dear heavenly Father,

I praise You, that You are perfect in Your discipline of Your children, that You only discipline us for our good (Hebrews 12:10) and never out of anger or spite. I honor Your Son for voluntarily submitting Himself to Your loving discipline to learn obedience even though He was without sin (Hebrews 5:8). Thank You that the fact that You discipline me demonstrates to me that I am a legitimate son of Yours (Hebrews 12:7-8) and that You discipline only those whom You love and accept as Your sons (Hebrews 12:5-6) just as I discipline only my own children.

But Father, I confess to You that at times I grumble and complain and feel that I have been dealt with unfairly by You. Other times I also admit that when I sin and don't experience immediate consequences I interpret this as "having gotten away with it." Oh Father, forgive me for making light of Your loving, patient discipline of me (Hebrews 12:5).

Thank You dear Lord, that You know perfectly how to discipline me. Thank You that you are never abusive or harsh in Your discipline of me but always gentle and compassionate. I don't receive the evil I deserve and I don't deserve the good things I continually receive from Your hand (Psalm 103:8-14).

You are perfectly consistent, dependable, and faithful in Your discipline, Father. Help me to see You afresh in Your commitment to make me like Your Son, Jesus (Hebrews 12:10). I trust that this, though painful for a while, produces a harvest of righteousness and peace in my life (Hebrews 12:11).

And Lord Jesus, will You please lead me and show me the balance of upholding Your holy standards and yet showing my children the same mercy and compassion that You show to me (Matthew 18:21-35).

In The Name of Jesus, my Good Shepherd, Amen.

TEACHING ARTICULATELY

"When I was a boy in my father's house, still tender and an only child of my mother, he taught me and said, 'Lay hold of my words with all your heart; keep my commands and you will live. Get wisdom, get understanding; do not forget my words or swerve from them'."

(Proverbs 4: 3-5 NIV)

School Involvement and Distorted Heavenly Father Images

A father who fails to be involved in teaching his children unintentionally teaches them that the heavenly Father is disinterested in the most significant part of their young lives. On the other hand, a father who overly focuses upon his children's performance in school teaches them that God is more interested in performance than relationship.

School is so much more for a child than academics. It is the place where he or she receives many messages about his/her value and worth. It is a place where he will be tempted to succumb to negative peer pressure, to cheat, or disrespect his teacher. The child of the uninvolved father will view God as one who is unwilling to enter into his world of school.

The father who obsesses over his child's school performance and grades portrays a God concerned with the external over the internal, the "bottom line" rather than One who takes joy in the journey together.

In both extremes a father is being selfish. The father who does not enter into his child's education is usually selfishly absorbed with his own world. The father who is overly concerned over his child's academic or athletic performance is often seeking to glorify himself through the reflected glory of his child's achievements. Both of these types of self-centeredness can profoundly impact a child's view of God, the heavenly Father.

Again, a father's extremes can have unhealthy spiritual effects upon a child. Of the two extremes, I believe most of us fathers in 21st century North America are in greater danger of under-involvement in our children's education.

The Problem Defined

Tragically, fathers are *not* as involved in their children's education as they could and should be and certainly not as much as their children's mothers. This is the sad conclusion of the massive study by the National Center for Education Statistics. To make this trend even more tragic is that all of the research points to the fact that fathers' involvement makes a significant positive difference in a child's education.

A National Center for Education Statistics study concluded that "half of students get mostly A's and enjoy, school according to their parents, when their fathers are highly involved in their schools compared to one-third of students when their fathers have low levels of involvement."[1]

A Department of Education study entitled, "Father Involvement in Children's Schools" has concluded that children whose fathers are involved in their schools experience:

- Better grades
- Lower likelihood of repeating a grade or being expelled or suspended
- Increased participation in extracurricular activities
- More enjoyment of school.[2]

Thorough surveys from the National Center For Fathering have found that forty percent of dads never read to their children, fifty-eight percent never volunteer at their child's school, seventy-seven percent never have lunch with their children at school and thirty-seven percent never visit their child's classroom.

Let's try to get a better understanding of how this happens.

What Keeps Fathers Uninvolved In Schools

Clearly it is a lost opportunity for fathers and children when fathers do not involve themselves in their children's education. But how has this come to be? In a real way, a father's lack of involvement in his child's education is often a symptom of a deeper problem; *many fathers do not have their hearts turned to their children.* And yet even when a father's heart is in the right place there still exists some practical barriers that can keep a dad from being involved with his children's schooling.

As mothers and fathers multi-task and divide up the parenting workload, the details of the children's schooling often fall to the mother since she is still considered to be the primary care-giver. And even when the mother works part-or full-time she is generally the one who takes on this responsibility. She is the one who is interfacing with the teachers and volunteering to help at school. Add to that the fact that most K-6th-grade teachers are women, education takes on a distinctly "feminine feel" in our culture.

As the school year begins it takes it quickly takes on a momentum of its own. Before a father realizes it, the academic year is nearly over before he has ever stepped into his child's classroom. Without ever being on campus, a dad cannot visualize what his child goes through on a day-to-day basis. He then does not know what kinds of questions to ask his child. And so, as time goes by, he feels increasingly out of touch.

"How was school today?" is the standard dad question. And, you guessed it—"Fine" is the universal kid answer. This apparent lack of interest by a father is hurtful to a child even though he or she may not be able to fully understand or articulate it. All that a child knows is her dad doesn't seem to care much about the most important part of her life.

Another explanation for low father involvement in their children's education has to do with how differently fathers and mothers teach children. There is evidence that suggests that fathers promote young children's intellectual and social development mostly through play, while a mother's teaching influence is exerted more through talking and caretaking. If this is the case, the school setting naturally fits more into a mother's teaching style than a father's. Combine this with the fact that women generally read more than men and you see why fathers mistakenly retreat from the academic world.

And then the "fatigue factor" and its effect on fathers regarding school involvement cannot be underestimated. Put aside the fact that women also become tired. In those homes where the father is the primary wage earner, the last thing he wants to have waiting for him when he comes home from working all day is a struggle with his children's homework.

Fathers have had their own fathers' attitudes about education passed onto them. Like father, like son. If a father did not value education he likely will project that same attitude onto his own children. Deep down, children know if their father values academic achievement. If a man's father did not value education then it is easy for a man, when he is a father, to adopt the same attitude despite all of the rational evidence presented to him to the contrary.

In this age of exploding information technology in which we live, formal education has a significant role to play in preparing our children to be successful in their futures. It is really sad to see so many fathers passing on this anti-education philosophy to the detriment of their children and grandchildren. Granted, traditional colleges and universities are not for everybody, and we need to be very aware of the dangers of secular-humanistic indoctrination there, but I have seen bright kids leave high school with limited career options because they learned from their fathers a lack of commitment to education early on. Like father, like son.

Involvement Provides Teaching Opportunities

Instead of looking at education superficially, as merely a means for economic and social advancement, fathers need to become involved in their children's education and to see this as an opportunity to teach them their values.

There are at least six such opportunities that becoming involved in his children's schooling provides for a father. If a father keeps these six opportunities in mind, he will see involvement in his children's education as a continuing opportunity to teach his children not just to be successful academically but how to succeed in life.

Teaching Respect for Authority

The first opportunity that getting involved with school provides a dad is a special context to teach children to respect authority. Fathers need to model to their children that a teacher's authority needs to be respected. Disrespect for Cindy was one attitude that I have never tolerated in my children. This is a value that my father taught me and one that we sought to instill in our children as early as possible. Once our children began school we explained to them that they were to respect their teachers as they would respect us. Very early in the game with each of our kids this was tested as we would hear tales of a teacher's actions that made her sound as evil as a third-world military dictator.

Of course we would not just accept our child's side of the story but would investigate the situation on our own and hear the teacher's side of the story as well. Nine times out of ten we came to understand that the teacher's demand was quite reasonable and our child was simply chaffing against the authority. Our children are not bad kids. They are simply sinful human beings who will naturally react against authority rather than submit to it.

These conflicts with authority can be good teaching opportunities for fathers. Teaching our children the benefits of submitting to the various authorities in their lives, even when those authorities may not seem to be reasonable people, is of the highest importance. Of course, children need to know that the teacher's authority is not absolute and they should never be compelled to do something that violates God's ultimate authority.

Truths from the following biblical passages need to be taught to our children:

"… Obey your earthly masters with respect and fear, and with sincerity of heart, just as you would obey Christ"

(Ephesians 6:5 NIV).

"Everyone must submit himself to the governing authorities for there is no authority except that which God has established"

(Romans 13:1 NIV).

"… Submit yourselves to your master with all respect, not only to those who are good and considerate, but also those who are harsh"

(1 Peter 2:18 NIV).

I have a daughter and a niece, both of whom are bright, talented, and energetic. They both became disillusioned with the teaching profession by their mid-twenties. There are several factors for this. For my daughter, the most difficult part of her job as a teacher was the constant challenge she faced from the parents of her kids. The mothers particularly seemed more concerned for their children's "self-esteem" rather than their character development. When my daughter discussed the behavior of the child with the parent, the parent would automatically sympathize with the child and then my daughter had two problems on her hands rather than just one!

These two young women's exodus from the teaching profession is not an isolated incident. Many are leaving teaching today. When a teacher is burdened with the responsibility of teaching a classroom of students and she is not given the corresponding authority to carry out that responsibility, her job is no longer a joy but becomes a heavy burden.

Cindy and I have experienced a few occasions where we honestly did feel that one of our kids was being treated unfairly. However, even as we dealt with those situations we were careful to preserve our kids' need to have respect for their teacher. It does them no good for us to buy into their already critical attitude. The immediate issue is secondary when it comes to our children learning to respect authority even when that authority appears unreasonable.

Here dads can use stories to relate to their children. What father has not had to deal with working for a boss who was unreasonable? Who of us has not had to follow through on a job even when he didn't agree with the boss' approach?

This is a tough concept to teach our children, but how valuable it is for them if it can be learned. Our submission to authority, our obedience even when we do not fully understand or even agree, is a priority lesson that God wants to teach His children. Consider how much He focused upon this in training of the nation of Israel. If it is important for our heavenly Father to teach *His children*, then it should be a priority for fathers to teach *their children*. Like Father, like son.

Teaching a Biblical Worldview

A second teaching opportunity for a father is to teach his children to learn to apply a biblical worldview to what they are learning. "The fear of the LORD is the beginning of knowledge, but fools despise wisdom and discipline" (Proverbs 1:7 NIV). "In Him (Christ) are hidden all the treasures of wisdom and knowledge" (Galatians 2:3 NIV).

Your children are deluged with information and new knowledge as soon as they enter school. It can be overwhelming and much of it will seem unconnected and random. It is each father's privilege to connect that new information to the heart of the heavenly Father, its very source. Every single subject reflects the Creator. Mathematics shows the Creator's amazing order and consistency. Science teaches about His diversity, unity, and infinite creativity. History teaches about God's sovereignty in human affairs. And on it goes in every subject.

If fathers are feeding regularly on God's Word then they will be able to infuse their children with a worldview that does not partition off the "sacred" from the "secular." All of life is seen as holy and God is in everything. C.S. Lewis spoke of a friend of his who said to him, "When I see the world I can't see God." He replied to his friend, "When I see the world, I cannot NOT see God." If fathers can, like Lewis, see God in everything, they will be addressing what is probably the number-one motivational problem their kids have in school. How many times have you heard, "What practical use will *this* subject ever be to me?" By reminding our children that all knowledge has the potential to give them greater insight into their heavenly Father and His Son, then we fuel their desire to learn more.

Teaching a Strong Work Ethic

A third teaching opportunity fathers have through educational involvement is to teach their children a strong work ethic. Our children will be faced with the lie that happiness is found in following the path of least resistance and taking on the least amount of responsibility. They will see their peers follow this road and seemingly enjoy life more. Those who work hard and achieve high grades are ridiculed in many settings as "nerds." This warped view is reinforced through the various media that encourage instant gratification and a sense of entitlement.

Through the challenges provided by their daily school curriculum, fathers can teach their children that joy is not found in doing the easy thing, or in doing just enough to get by, but in doing their best, in persevering, denying themselves, and delaying short-term gratification to achieve a long-term goal.

In our family we have a little tradition called "The Red Plate." When one of our children accomplishes something academically for example he or she is able to eat off the red plate. It is a sign of special achievement, though this doesn't always mean getting an "A." One of my sons struggled throughout his academic career with a learning challenge. He worked very hard in high school to pull himself from a C/D student up to an A/B student. When he began to get B's we pulled out the red plate! I repeatedly told him a quote from Booker T. Washington, who said, "A man's greatness is not in what he achieves but in what he overcomes to achieve."

I have discovered that once our children taste that sense of accomplishment they crave for more. They are no longer satisfied with mediocrity. They desire to experience again that joy of doing their best academically. Our job as fathers is to be highlighters who highlight what our children feel to be true but need a confirmation from someone else so they can trust that it is indeed true. Children intuitively feel their own satisfaction, but they also greatly benefit from their father's reinforcement. A father's approval is so important because, remember, there is no one else in the world they would rather have be proud of them!

Teaching Honesty

A fourth teaching opportunity is for a father to teach his children the importance of honesty and integrity. In school there are many temptations to cut corners. There is the temptation to copy another's homework, to cheat on a test, to lie about the reasons that homework was not completed. That old dog that ate our homework is still roaming kids' bedrooms today! As our culture has moved away from teaching absolutes, children quickly learn to justify their wrong-doing with endless excuses.

Cindy, and I have prayed for our children that if they start to do something they shouldn't be doing that they would get caught early on so they won't become successful at lying and deception. God has been faithful to answer that prayer for each of our children.

Our oldest daughter, who has grown into a beautiful young mother, went through a period in junior high and early high school when she pushed and broke through some of the boundaries that were set for her. One day she decided with her friends that, against the school's rules, they would leave campus. And sure enough, Heidi "just happened" to be spotted by the school's vice-principal who "just happened" to have left campus on an errand that day. And when she first started driving and was driving too fast one day, our faithful car insurance agent spotted her on the road and called to let us know. Our daughter may have escaped the long arm of the law but not the roving eyes of the Lord!

For some kids honesty is not an issue, but for others it is. School experiences will test your children in this area. What you want them to realize is that they have a chance to build a record of trustworthiness. When they are honest with you then that builds trust. This is the gradual opening of a child's "box" that surrounds them and protects them until they have proven the can handle more freedom, as discussed in the discipline chapter. The box will open gradually as they prove themselves trustworthy. The rate of opening of the box depends upon them. When they are caught in a deception, as our daughter was in those situations, the box stays the same size for a while.

Teaching about Success and Failure

Another opportunity that a father has is to teach his children about how God views success and failure. We live in a world that glorifies success, celebrity status, and winning at all costs. Children without strong parental input can mistakenly see themselves as "losers" early on in life. They are bombarded with media images of success and do not see the many failures that so-called successful people have experienced on the road to their "overnight success."

In school our children are measured against each other academically, athletically, socially, and in just about every other way. I remember when our youngest daughter was chosen to represent her fourth grade class in a spelling bee. She had only moderately practiced her list of words before the contest and perhaps she could have prepared for it a bit more. She was the very first one to sit down that day. In case you are wondering, with spelling bees, being "first" is not a good thing.

Even though I think that I would have misspelled the word she was given that day, she was crushed by the humiliation of being the first one out. I tried to comfort her but that made her even more upset. So I just decided to ride it out. Eventually she gained her equilibrium and talked about putting more preparation in next year and that she was going to go much further in the competition.

Just about a week later I had the opportunity to talk to her class and the teacher asked me, "What one thing about Holly are you most proud?" It came right to my mind, how she handled the disappointment in the spelling bee. I used her as an example of how to handle failure and disappointment as part of becoming a successful person. Failure is something we just do not seem to talk about enough in our culture. Yet it is a natural, healthy part of life. God's Word teaches us that it is what we do with failure that determines our character, not whether we fail or not.

As I reflect upon my childhood I can remember how I dreaded failure and I could not stand for my father to see me in a situation where he would see me fail. If I failed to perform in some athletic situation in front of him, whether it was dropping a fly ball, dropping a baton in a relay race or striking out, I could not stand to face him afterwards. And, yes, I did all three of these things at one time or another while he was watching. I did not know how to deal with it when I failed in athletics or in other endeavors. Even though this was an irrational belief, I saw my father as a person who had not failed as I failed and one who would not want to relate to me at those times because of my failure.

Being an involved father in our children's school provides a golden opportunity to teach our kids about success and failure. Success is *doing one's best, not necessarily being the best*. The Bible says that success is doing whatever we do "heartily as unto the Lord, and not as unto men" (Colossians 3:23 NIV).

Theodore Roosevelt summed up the true philosophy of success and failure when he wrote, "Far better is it to dare mighty things, to win glorious triumphs, even though checkered by failure... than to rank with those poor spirits who neither enjoy nor suffer much, because they live in a gray twilight that knows not victory nor defeat."

Failure only occurs when we do not try, when we quit and give up. Fathers who instill this philosophy will tend to produce courageous children who are willing to step out and take risks. Another quote which I have come to appreciate is this, from an anonymous source, "The boat in the harbor is safe, but that is not what boats are built for." I have to say that my father did model to me a man willing to risk, to seek, to do big things, even if that means occasionally failing. I can remember him warning me when I was young, "No matter whatever else you do in life, don't become a critic. Do something, anything, but don't criticize those who try." Also, when we went into a restaurant venture in Hawaii together he would say, "We're going to give it our best. If we fail, we're going down in flames."

Dads, if there ever was a time in history when young people need to be raised up unafraid to risk and to fail, now is the time. May this generation be raised up unafraid, willing to risk great things for God and His kingdom!

Teaching Kindness and Encouragement

We live in a self-centered world, and children can be cruel. They can be ruthless in the way that they put down each other. Often as we ask our kids about their day Cindy or I will ask them, "Did you encourage anyone today?" Or "Were you kind to someone today?" Even if their answer is something like, "I dunno," by continually asking our kids these questions, we reinforce to them that this is what we value as a family, even more than academic achievement. As the Bible says, "knowledge puffs up, but love builds up" (1 Corinthians 8:1 NIV).

One day I noticed that our junior high son had befriended some kids at school who were quieter, who were not athletic, and perhaps not from the "cool group" at school. I strongly affirmed him for it and reminded him that this is pleasing to God. Besides, I jokingly added, he may be working for one of those guys someday!

These six values can all be taught to our children as we are involved with their formal education. Our children will spend 180 days a year at school for thirteen of the eighteen years they live in your home. That is about six hours every day that they are being impacted by other kids and by teachers who may have different values and goals than we have. With this in mind we need to be looking proactively to impart our values to them through the crucible of their education experience.

Practically Helping Kids Succeed in School

Here are a half dozen suggestions for dads about how to get involved with their children's school experience.

1. **Read with your kids** - This is something that we should begin when they are little. Teach them the love of reading. Here fathers can be great models by having their kids just watching them read. So much of school success involves reading. My wife is great about taking the children to the library and checking out books for them to read. Our family has a couple of mottos: "We're a reading family, " and "Leaders are readers."

2. **Establish a daily routine** -Decide with your wife about the time for homework and the time to turn off the TV. Some families don't allow TV or non-school computer use on school nights. We allow about an hour . The younger kids are supposed to go to bed at 8:30 or 9. We don't let the children wait until late in the night to start their homework. We find it gets to be 9:30 or 10 and then they want our help. By that time, I am not a happy camper. In fact I let them know that their mom and I are "Off Duty" when it gets too far into the evening.

3. **Make the most of bedtime** - This is a golden opportunity to talk with your children about school. This is a time when they are motivated to talk. This may not last into the teen years, but when they are young it is an opportunity for them to recount the school day to us.

4. **Visit the campus as much as possible** -There are numerous opportunities to be involved with our children at school. It is so important to go on a field trip if we can or take a day or a half day to spend with them. When we are on their turf just one time early in the school year we are able to ask better questions and visualize what their day is like. It really helps. We are able to see them in social situations and know what they need to work on. Plus our presence says to them, "Wow, my education is important to my Dad!" Going to the campus enabled us to know that we needed to pull our oldest son out of one school. And our campus presence also helped us to make a decision about our youngest son and a needed school change.

5. **Help with homework** - Work with your wife as your teammate. It is important that you are on the same page as your wife when it comes to school. Homework help is a true balancing act. You will have to devise your own division of labor. But here is a practical way to work together that Cindy and I use. In our family our kids know that after about third grade they don't come to me for math help. But I can be helpful to them in English, history and Bible. Mom handles all the forms and paperwork. They know better than to give that stuff to me. I help my kids with homework when I feel they have already made an honest effort and they just need a little help, when they want

me to read or edit a paper, listen as they practice a presentation, help them memorize something, or quiz them for a test. I do not help them when they haven't done any work on their own, when they come to me late at night, or when they want me to do the work for them.

6. **Connect With your child's teacher** - Parent-teacher conferences are not just for Mom. They are where you make a good initial contact and then you can use email as a good tool to keep up the communication. You want your children's teachers to know that you are concerned about your child's education and social development and are available to be emailed if there are any concerns. One thing that I have learned from parent-teacher conferences: "If I don't take too much credit when they do well, I won't have to take too much blame when they don't."

A Father's Prayer of Transformation

Dear Father, I give You praise for Your constant teaching, counseling and guiding me by Your precious Holy Spirit (Psalm 25:8-10). I praise You for the Counselor You have sent to me through Your Son to guide me into all truth (John 16:12-13). I love You for being a God who is truly interested in teaching me and shaping me through all of my life's experiences, that You always have the goal in Your mind to conform me to become like Jesus. I praise You that You have given me the mind of Christ (1 Corinthians 2:16) to enable me to understand Your very heart!

Father, as I consider myself a teacher of my children, I confess to You that much of what I teach them is not from You. I have allowed my thinking to be conformed to the world's way of thinking (Romans 12:2) as I have been more concerned about their bottom-line performance and not that they are molded into the image of Your dear Son (Romans 8:28-29). At times I have been lazy and not been engaged in their life at school, too caught up in my needs and my challenges. Forgive me and help me to change by taking practical steps towards greater school involvement.

Thank You for my children's school, their teachers, coaches and all the help You have lovingly placed in their lives so they can learn. Help me to team with them but not to give over their education to these people.

Lord Jesus, I offer myself anew to You so that You may teach my children knowing that my competency to teach them anything comes from YOU and not myself (2 Corinthians 3:5-6). Use this cracked clay pot to impart to them the eternal treasure of knowing You (2 Corinthians 4:7).

In the name of Jesus my Teacher, Amen

SECTION 3

CONNECTING TO YOUR CHILD'S HEART—MEETING EMOTIONAL NEEDS

Meeting physical needs is important, but many men have grown up with a father who did that yet they still feel a deep void inside left over from the relationship. Though such things as investing time, actively listening, cultivating awareness, and showing affection may not be as "quantifiable" as putting a roof over our family's head or helping our kids succeed in school, it is not any less important. In fact, it can be argued that if a father meets physical needs without connecting to his child's heart he has really missed the mark as a dad.

Learning to connect with our child's heart, with meeting emotional needs, often comes out of our own trial and error failures. Many fathers did not have this taught or modeled to them by their fathers, so for many it is like being right-handed and having to learn to throw a ball with the left hand.

We mistakenly equate what cannot be measured (i.e., meeting our children's emotional needs) for what is not significant. We could not be more wrong. All we have to do is to think back to what we needed from our fathers. Most would not say that "he worked harder and earned more money" but would instead say things like, "for my dad to have hung out with me more" or "for my dad to have really listened to me more."

Let me tell you about a father who has taught me much in this area of emotional connecting, particularly in the area of listening. This man is my former pastor, Brad, the man most used by God to save my marriage and family during our "eighth year rash." First, he patiently listened to me in those difficult days when I just needed to vent my anger and frustration. He was very "unpreacher-like" as he empathized, listened, and realized what I needed most from him at that time. Brad would be the first to admit that he has not been a perfect father. In fact, he would tell you that he has learned more about the heart of the heavenly Father through his struggles than from when he did things "right."

He and his wife, Anita, have three birth-sons, two adopted daughters and one adopted son with special needs. What I respect most about Brad is his willingness to listen, to receive correction even when it comes from one of his own children.

Brad has said that as a pastor and a father, "The battle for me was between two things that I loved, my job and my family. It wasn't between two things I hated; it was between two things I loved and had to balance out."

The pendulum of "balance" naturally was not always right in the middle where it should be, so Brad occasionally needed to be willing to listen to his own children's (and wife's) gentle rebukes. He recalls his oldest son pulling him aside one day when he began to let slip the time he was spending with his growing sons. His son said to him, "Dad, I hope you can make more of the games for my brothers than you have for me." Brad remembers, "It made me aware that my commitment had slipped and that I needed to turn my heart more towards my kids."

Several years later, when Brad had taken on a supervisory job of pastors which demanded even more time away from home than his previous pastorate had, that same son came to him and said, "You know, Dad, you have always told me not to be too busy for the important things in life. And for the most part you have been really good about that, but lately I don't feel like you are here for Mom or the rest of us. We miss you."

Brad listened and corrected his course. You may know that a jet plane when making a trip from one city to another is off course ninety percent of the time. The reason the plane gets to the destination is that the pilot is constantly making corrections. Over the years, Brad has been willing to listen to his family and correct his course.

What is admirable about Brad is how he has taken the hurts and heartaches of his own fathering journey and allowed them to lead him to know more deeply the heart of the heavenly Father. He recalls, "I can remember one time I was telling God how frustrated I was with one of my kids. I could then hear God say to me in my spirit, "It's a good thing you only have one. I have millions!" He has allowed his pain to be a point of personal identification with his loving heavenly Father.

Brad continues, "[The heavenly Father] experiences frustration with us all the time. He doesn't complain. He doesn't abandon us. He doesn't come down on us in a ridiculing way. He patiently rebukes and disciplines. So these experiences as a father have actually deepened my relationship with God."

The struggle in learning to connect to the hearts of his children has drawn Brad to connect with the heart of Another Father. Increasingly Brad can say, by God's grace he is becoming more like his heavenly Father. "Like Father, like son."

Chapter 7

INVESTING TIME

"These commandments that I give you today are to be upon your hearts. Impress them on your children. Talk about them when you sit at home and when you walk along the road, when you lie down and when you get up."

(Deuteronomy 6:6-7 NIV)

Investment of Time and Distorted Heavenly Father Images

I can remember spending a day with my dad when I was about three or four years old. He was running errands and, with a little nudging from his tired wife, he took me along. He kept me motivated throughout the day because he told me that when we were finished he would show me the biggest tree in Santa Barbara. Little did he know that every tree that I saw as we drove all day through a city filled with trees I would ask, "Is that it, Dad?" Finally, when his errands had been run and he was thoroughly worn out by my constant questioning, "Is that it, dad?" he showed me this historic old oak tree down by the railroad tracks. But I felt deceived as I saw that tree and I said, "Dad, that's not the biggest tree in Santa Barbara; that's just the fattest."

I remember that day almost a half a century later, because I spent the entire day with my dad…just him and me, one on one. What we did was not that important. What *was* important was that we were together.

A child who does not have a father who invests time with him will tend to project a feeling onto God, the heavenly Father, that He is not present as well. A dad who reluctantly spends time with his children will be found out. He teaches his children unwittingly that God also resents spending time with them. I have found that many people today, both men and women, have an easier time believing that God *loves* them than also believing that God *likes* them, that is He enjoys just being with them.

Where does that come from? Could it originate from the impression that many of us as fathers give to our children that we would rather be doing anything else but spending time with them? How many times do we convey the feeling that we would rather be somewhere else?

Maybe the problem with not investing time with our children is that we forget that the time we have together is very precious. As an older, wiser father warned a younger father, "You'd better slow down and look behind you so you can see what your future is going to be like."

Historically, father involvement, the amount of time a dad spends with his children, is the determining factor in the quality of the relationship he has with his children. When the amount of time a father spends with his children is increased, the father-child bond generally becomes stronger. We have all heard that children spell love: "T-I-M-E."

But most dads today feel the tremendous pressure of 21st century life and its accelerated pace. Forty hours each week at work is not enough; jobs demand attention, and for many it is fifty, sixty hours or even more. Kids often put in hours of homework, or spend extra hours working on developing their proficiency in a sport, or in developing a talent or skill. Wives who need to work half or full-time find the little discretionary time they do have being used up in the mindless watching of television just to decompress from the demands of the day. Then everyone goes to bed and does it all over again the next day. It has been rightly said, "Busyness isn't of the devil; busyness is the devil!"

The Time Squeeze

A study was conducted to determine the amount of interaction between middle- class fathers and their small children. First, the fathers were asked to estimate the amount of time they spent each day with their children. The average time spent was about fifteen to twenty minutes. Next, microphones were attached to the father so that each interaction during the day could be recorded. The results of the study were shocking. The average amount of time these fathers spent with their children was thirty-seven seconds per day. Their direct interaction was limited to 2.7 encounters daily, lasting ten to fifteen seconds each![1]

A Story about the Value of Time Spent

Just as my father probably thought nothing of the time that he spent with me that day in my young life so many years ago, the problem may be that we simply underestimate the power of investing time. Here's a story from an unknown source sent to me by a friend:

It had been some time since Jack had seen the old man. College, girls, career, and life itself got in the way. In fact, Jack had moved clear across the country in pursuit of his dreams.

There, in the rush of his busy life, Jack had little time to think about the past and often no time to spend with those important to him. He was working on his future, and nothing could stop him.

Over the phone, his mother told him, "Mr. Belser died last night. The funeral is Wednesday." Memories flashed through his mind like an old newsreel as he sat quietly remembering his childhood days. "Jack, did you hear me?"

"Oh, sorry, Mom. Yes, I heard you. It's been so long since I thought of him. I'm sorry, but I honestly thought he died years ago," Jack said.

"Well, he didn't forget you. Every time I saw him he'd ask how you were doing. He'd reminisce about the many days you spent over "his side of the fence" as he put it," Mom told him.

"I loved that old house he lived in," Jack said. "You know, Jack, after your father died, Mr.Belser stepped in to make sure you had a man's influence in your life," she said. "He's the one who taught me carpentry," Jack said. "I wouldn't be in this business if it weren't for him. He spent a lot of time teaching me things he thought were important...Mom, I'll be there for the funeral," Jack said.

As busy as he was, he kept his word. Jack caught the next flight to his hometown. Mr. Belser's funeral was small and uneventful. He had no children of his own, and most of his relatives had passed away. The night before he had to return home, Jack and his Mom stopped by to see the old house next door one more time.

Standing in the doorway, Jack paused for a moment. It was like crossing over into another dimension, a leap through space and time. The house was exactly as he remembered it. Every step held memories. Every picture, every piece of furniture...Jack stopped suddenly. "What's wrong, Jack?" his Mom asked. "The box is gone," he said. "What box? " Mom asked. "There was a small gold box that he kept locked on top of his desk. I must have asked him a thousand times what was inside. All he'd ever tell me was 'the thing I value most,'" Jack said. It was gone.

Everything about the house was exactly how Jack remembered it, except for the box. He figured someone from the Belser family had taken it. "Now I'll never know what was so valuable to him," Jack said. "I better get some sleep. I have an early flight home, Mom." It had been about two weeks since Mr. Belser died. Returning home from work one day Jack discovered a note in his mailbox. "Signature required on a package. No one at home. Please stop by the main post office within the next three days," the note read.

Early the next day Jack retrieved the package. The small box was old and looked like it had been mailed a hundred years ago. The handwriting was difficult to read, but the return address caught his attention. "Mr. Harold Belser" it read. Jack took the box out to his car and ripped open the package. There inside was the gold box and an envelope. Jack's hands shook as he read the note inside.

"Upon my death, please forward this box and its contents to Jack Bennett. It's the thing I valued most in my life." A small key was taped to the letter. His heart racing, as tears filled his eyes, Jack carefully unlocked the box. There inside he found a beautiful gold pocket watch. Running his fingers slowly over the finely etched casing, he unlatched the cover. Inside he found these words engraved: "Jack, Thanks for your time!-Harold Belser."

"The thing he valued most...was...my time."

Jack held the watch for a few minutes, then called his office and cleared his appointments for the next two days. "Why?" Janet, his assistant, asked.

"I need some time to spend with my son," he said. "Oh, by the way, Janet...thanks for your time!"

The Scriptural View of Time

Since there is a crisis in America in the amount of time that fathers are spending with their children and time invested is what communicates love from fathers to children, then it should come as no surprise that children today are not feeling loved. Before taking a look at how this can be turned around, let's see how the concept of time is pictured in the Bible. In the Scriptures time is seen as opportunity. When you consider time as something that is neutral, like money, that can be invested for good, evil, or squandered, then I think you are able to better understand how time is seen from God's perspective.

In Psalm 90:10,12 NIV, Moses wrote: "The length of our days is seventy years—or eighty, if we have strength: yet their span is but trouble and sorrow, for they quickly pass away...teach us to number our days aright, that we may gain a heart of wisdom."

Time, which is fleeting so quickly, needs to be treasured and considered as extremely valuable. How one lives every day is important so that every day is lived with purpose. The goal for a person of faith is to gain a heart of wisdom or grow in godly character during our fleeting days on this earth so that he or she is pleasing to God.

The apostle Paul picks up on this opportunity idea when he writes, "Be careful, then, how you live—not as unwise but as wise, making the most of every opportunity because the days are evil. Therefore, do not be foolish but understand what the Lord's will is" (Ephesians 5:15-17 NIV). The word for time here is from the Greek word "Kairos" which indicates quality of time, as opposed to "Chronos" which means quantity of time. That is why this is translated as "opportunity" in English. Paul indicates that unless a person makes a conscious choice, a top-of-the-mind kind of decision to live with wisdom and to capture the opportunities he has been provided, then the opportunities will be lost, squandered, and will default to evil.

To not make the most of opportunities is like fumbling the ball when your football team has driven down the field and is ready to score. It is like leaving ten men stranded on base in a 2-1 loss in baseball. It is like missing two free throws when your basketball team is down by one point with no time left on the clock. You get the idea. When you do not make a positive choice to capture opportunity in the spiritual realm you are sure to lose because the "default switch" in our fallen world always goes in the direction of evil and loss.

Paul underlines this truth as he writes, urging his readers to receive God's grace: Though our days are brief they are not unimportant. In fact this short life we are given is of eternal significance! "I tell you now is the time of God's favor, now is the day of salvation" (2 Corinthians 6:2 NIV).

Then the Lord Jesus Christ Himself, when He was in the process of healing a blind man, taught us that time is opportunity. "As long as it is day, we must do the work of him who sent Me. Night is coming, when no one can work. While I am in the world, I am the light of the world" (John 9:4 NIV).

Again we see Jesus confirming the biblical view of time. Time is short, fleeting but important. He sees it as something that must be captured for the Father's use, as there will be a day when this season of opportunity to do the Father's work will be over. There will come a "darkness" when people's eternal fates will be sealed and opportunities for response to God's grace will no longer exist.

Now let's take this view of time and apply it to fathering. To not make a decision to invest time in your children's life equals a decision to not invest time that will never return. It takes a conscious choice to make the most of an opportunity and not squander it. Even in those spontaneous situations a father needs to have his heart turned toward his children in order for that time to be translated for good.

There is no guarantee that you or your children will be able to spend eighteen years of life under your roof. Divorce, tragic accidents, or illnesses can take away the time you thought you had coming with your kids. Even in the best of circumstances, as our children move into adolescence and greater independence, time together becomes increasingly hard to find. "The Perfect Storm" of lost opportunity often occurs when a father's career efforts are at their very highest and his children hit the teen years.

We have to face the hard facts. If we do nothing proactively when it comes to time investment in our children's lives, if we just "go with the flow," we will lose. Whether we realize it or not, we are in a war with a very real enemy who wants to steal our time from our children, kill opportunities that we have to teach our faith, values, and very heart and destroy the potential for lasting memories with a loving father (see John 10:10).

We can either accept this reality and live accordingly or choose to disbelieve it and go our merry way. To believe this message means that we will continually need to be willing to change and adjust our lives, which is not "comfortable."

Let's Take a Look At Jesus

Perhaps there has not been a more "time-challenged" person in human history than Jesus of Nazareth. It is important to remember that Jesus, though not a biological father, was a spiritual father to his twelve disciples whom He called to be with Him for the three years of His public ministry (Mark 3:14). If we look at a couple of events in our Lord's life with new eyes we will see something which can be called "multipurposing." This is different from multitasking. Multitasking is best modeled for us today by the man listening on his cell phone, with one hand on the steering wheel of his car, while he desperately tries with the other to jot down a note in his palm pilot, all the while trying to carry on an intelligent conversation with his teenager in the front seat of his car. If you think I am being judgmental here, I just described myself!

Multipurposing is doing one task at a time but doing that one task with two or more purposes. Jesus is never seen multitasking but repeatedly we can see him "multipurposing."

The key thing to remember when we look at Jesus in the Gospel accounts is that He never stopped being a father to His men. He integrated His fathering into everything He did. In other words, when He was dealing with any one situation He did not screen out His relationship with His disciples, He did not try to "compartmentalize." He drew them into whatever He was doing as the Father was leading Him. This integrated approach to life was summarized by Jesus Himself when He said, "My Father is always at his work to this very day, and I, too am working" (John 5:19 NIV).

In the encounter that Jesus had with the Samaritan woman recorded in John chapter four, think of all that He accomplished through the one simple act of sitting by a well in Sychar, Samaria. He broke down racial, gender, religious and lifestyle barriers by engaging in conversation with a Samaritan woman who was likely an outcast in her own town. He revealed His Messiahship to her and she, in turn, revealed it to the townspeople. He revealed His heart to His disciples when they offered Him food and He replied, "My food is to do the will of Him who sent Me and to finish His work" (John 4:34 NIV).

While sitting by Jacob's well and resting and carrying on a conversation with a Samaritan woman, Jesus was modeling a lesson to His spiritual children that they would never forget. He rested, had a deep impact on one woman, planted the seed of the gospel in Samaria, and taught His disciples what was on His heart all in one motion. He was never hurried or stressed out. He simply captured the opportunities.

A little later as recorded in the Gospel of John, Jesus taught a multitude of people (John 6). A crowd of about 5,000 people came to Him, it says, "because they had seen His miraculous signs." Even with the people crowding in on Him, the text indicates that Jesus knew all along what He intended to do. But as a model father He was always involving, engaging, and stretching the faith of His spiritual children.

Jesus then asked where bread might be bought to feed the crowd. Philip responded that it would be impossible to come up with enough money to feed the crowd. Jesus then accepted what was given to them by a small boy who had a small lunch of two small fish and five barley loaves. Jesus then involved His disciples in the miracle by having them help distribute the bread and later collect the leftovers. Again Jesus integrated the miraculous meeting of the crowd's need with the teaching and training of His disciples.

These are just two examples of this time-challenged Man's ability to live unhurried and at peace because He focused upon doing the Father's will by making the most of every opportunity He was given. He could confidently say to His Father at the end of His earthly life that He had completed His work (John 17:4). He carried His fathering role to the very end, praying this prayer just hours before His crucifixion, no doubt in the Apostle John's presence. It is also amazing that on the cross Jesus did a very fatherly thing for His mother, Mary. He entrusted her into the hands of His most beloved disciple, John (John 19:26-27). Now that is multipurposing!

Living Like Jesus

So how does this multipurposing concept work for those of us who are human, as Jesus is, but do not also possess deity? Moses gives the Great Commandment in the book of Deuteronomy, "Hear, O Israel: The LORD our God, the LORD is one. Love the LORD your God with all your heart and with all your soul and with all your strength. These commandments that I give you today are to be upon your hearts" (Deuteronomy 6:4-6 NIV). So it is "job one" for a father to have a love relationship with God and His Word. But look further to see how a father is called to pass this love relationship on to his children.

"Impress them on your children. Talk about them when you sit at home and when you walk along the road, and when you lie down and when you get up" (Deuteronomy 6:7 NIV). This is multipurposing. When a dad is hanging out at home he is also teaching God's truth. When he is walking (or today driving) with his kids, he is teaching them. When he is putting them to bed and when he is getting them going in the morning, he is always responsible to make the most of every opportunity to communicate God's truth to them. He never stops fathering.

What about the father who must spend large quantities of time away from home in order to provide for his family? Time that a father spends away out of necessity is still time invested in his children. He works in order to meet his children's needs. The Scriptures say, "If anyone does not provide for his relatives, and especially for his immediate family, he has denied the faith and is worse than an unbeliever" (1 Timothy 5:8 NIV). The father in these times of necessity should not judge himself with feelings of guilt that he is not spending the time other fathers are able to spend with their children. The issue is always the heart. Each of us must search our own heart in this matter. Is the issue about meeting my family's needs or is it about something else? There is also the case of the non-custodial father. His decision to provide and to do the right thing despite a lack of continual time with his children is a high and noble calling to fulfill.

Specific Applications of This Concept

Most fathers are unable to make any significant reductions in their work hours or change schedules all at once. If you are frustrated about the lack of time being invested in your children's lives, how can you begin to turn this Titanic around? You simply need to begin to look with different eyes at what you already do and what your kids are doing.

Here are a few examples: Starting with your work, it may be impossible to bring your children to your workplace but you can have reminders of them with you in picture form. I have heard of men who travel who take photos of their wife and children with them and set them up in their hotel room. You can use your phone and email to keep connected. My thirteen-year-old daughter is an "IM (Instant Message) maniac." I hate instant messages because they are such an interruption but I have learned to go back and forth with her because IM is speaking her language of connection. (She tells me I am funnier on IM than in real life) When my oldest daughter was in college, emails connected us almost daily. Emails don't work with my son at college so I have tried using the phone. The point is, as long as I am faithful to accomplish my job I make a point to find moments in the day to stay connected to my kids.

Don't forget to call your wife during the day just to touch base and ask how her day is going. Not every work situation allows this, but I have found that, when it is possible, it is a great way to keep the family "top of mind" even while not being physically present at home.

How about doing chores around the house or the yard? Many father's weekends are taken up by chores—you know, the infamous "Honey Do List." I have been blessed with a wife who is more mechanically inclined and who also happens to be a gardener so I hit the jackpot there. But I still do get my opportunities. Why not take the time to do a chore alongside one of your kids, taking the time to teach them a little at a time what you are doing? Isn't it cute to see little kids following their dads around holding a hammer? My oldest daughter used to follow Cindy around with a hammer (I told you I'm a lucky guy!).

The heavenly Father has placed within children, especially sons, this desire to mimic their dads at work. Doing this will slow you down and you may not finish in that session, but what an opportunity to connect with your kids! Sometimes when the kids are little you have to make up jobs for them to do. One dad told me that with one of his kids he gave him the job of keeping the dog out of the garage while he was working. Sounds like a good job to me.

And what about those hobbies and sports that you love to do on the weekends? The question is, do they really help make us better dads? Do they help strengthen family relationships or are they just another way to escape? Are they connectors or things that will create barriers? In each season, ask yourself what can be done together? I have found that in the summer a lazy trip down one of the Puget Sound's Cascade rivers on one of my sit-on-top kayaks is a lot of fun to do with my kids. In the winter, skiing and snowboarding are what our kids enjoy doing together. Whatever sport our kids are in is an opportunity to shoot hoops, play catch or kick the ball around together. Look at the ages of your kids, your finances, activities in your area, and take the lead in planning some fun things to do as a family. You will find it well worth it.

And finally, what about family entertainment (television, DVD's, movies and music)? Yes, it is sad that in the 1950s the American family stopped talking around the dinner table and started to congregate around the television. But the family is at far greater risk today when it comes to spending quality time together. Many homes have multiple television sets that present multiple entertainment options, especially for children and youth. We have family members individually consuming entertainment with no connection to one another. Dad, there are great opportunities here. Go rent a family-friendly DVD and have a "Family Movie Night" complete with popcorn for everybody. Afterwards you can lead a discussion as a family of the theme, either formally or informally, whatever you feel is appropriate for your family.

Up to this point we have concentrated on how we fathers invite our children into *our* world. But what about the ways we can become more involved in *their* world?

School is the obvious place to start, as we have previously discussed. As mentioned in the last chapter, you can get involved by volunteering one day per semester or one day during the school year. This pays huge dividends in understanding what goes on in your children's daily lives. In the elementary years, teachers are often in need of parents to help with field trips. How about you, Dad?

What about helping with the carpool? It is interesting that as my kids got into their adolescent years we entered the period of one word answers. They suddenly became monosyllabic around me. "How was your day?" The reply was predictably, "Fine." But when they were in the car with their friends or someone of approximately the same age they would begin to talk. By driving them to places, I found that I could crash the party by getting involved in those conversations. Often I was also able to send them off to school with a prayer. And if you have children who want help with homework, consider this an engraved invitation to enter into their world.

Keep an eye on their entertainment. As parents we need to be aware of what our children are watching or listening to. It is important to have communicated standards. But what I am talking about is taking advantage of opportunities to watch with them or listen to what they like with them. Often the things that we approve of they would not be interested in because it is not geared to their age range. I can recall going to a three-day outdoor summer concert with my son. It was a kind of "Christian Woodstock" for teens called Creation 2000 and was held in George, Washington. The music was not my favorite, but it was what he enjoyed and it was time well spent together.

Take an active interest in their sports activities. This is where many dads can easily spend much time with their kids, playing catch, shooting baskets, kicking balls, or whatever else we come up with to help them develop their athletic skills. I have spent countless hours rebounding basketballs and throwing baseballs with my sons. The thing I always have to remind myself is that this is not about making my sons into professional athletes. It is about spending time together. The danger I have fallen into is that my focus becomes too intense and too performance-oriented and less about play.

As I reflect upon my fathering, I can see on the one hand that I did integrate and multipurpose more than I thought I did, and I am thankful for that. But I do feel some regret over the times I allowed my work to invade my home life. Also there are too many times when I escaped into my little cocoon of personal comfort and watched television alone. More than once I said to my kids that I was too tired to play catch that night. All of those are opportunities lost.

It all comes down to making conscious choices. One conscious choice that every father can make is to choose to have a personal date with each of his children. This can be weekly or monthly, whatever is practical for the father and each child. In our family we call this "Face Time." This is a time that each of our kids can have one-on-one time with Dad usually once a month. What we do during that time varies, but the important thing is that as father and son or father and daughter we do something together that they want to do. This has meant a trip to the mall or a bike ride, an excursion to the zoo, a ball game, or a movie. It always includes eating together. Just spending TIME together is all that really matters. Put it on your calendar and make it happen!

A Father's Prayer of Transformation

Dear Father,

I praise You that are a God who has all of the time in the world for every one of Your children, as if each of us were the only ones in all of creation You were concerned about. I love You, Father, for not just loving me but for liking me, wanting to be with me. You delight in spending time with me, even rejoicing over me with singing (Zephaniah 3:17). I praise You, Lord that Your very name, Emmanuel, means "God with us" (Matthew 1:23). I praise You that there is nowhere I could ever escape on earth from Your loving presence (Psalm 139).

But Father, I confess that my picture of You is different from what You reveal of Yourself through Your word. I find it hard to believe that You actually enjoy spending time with me. I can't help feeling that You surely must want to spend Your time somewhere else than with me. I have difficulty believing that You eagerly await our special times together in Your Word and prayer. Lord, I want to see more clearly that You are with me always throughout every part of my day.

Lord, I do believe that You are with me, but help me to overcome my unbelief (Matthew 9:24). I thank You for the privilege I have to invest time in my children. I thank You for what they teach me about the simple joy of being together. They are very important in Your eyes and the time I invest in them is eternally significant (Matthew 18:10). Thank You for revealing this to me before it was too late.

Father, will You enable me to offer my family the greatest gift that I can offer—myself and my time. Teach me to number my days so that when they are done I will have gained a heart of wisdom (Psalm 90:12). Lord, teach me the reality that the days I live in are slanted toward evil and loss unless I choose to take the opportunities to invest in my family members' lives for Your purposes (Ephesians 5:15-16).

At the end of my life I long to say like Jesus, "I have brought You glory on earth by completing the work You gave me to do" (John 17:4).

In The name Of Jesus, the eternal I AM, Amen.

Chapter 8

ACTIVELY LISTENING

"My dear brothers, take note of this: Everyone should be quick to listen, slow to speak and slow to become angry, for man's anger does not bring about the righteous life that God desires"

(James 1:19-20 NIV).

The Listening Lack and Distorted Heavenly Father Images

There are definite spiritual implications for a father who does not actively listen to his children. It is reasonable to believe that children with a non-listening father will grow up "seeing" God as one who is not eager to hear them in prayer but rather a God who is distracted and disengaged. These children may see God as one who wants to speak to them but who is not very interested in listening to them. After all, why would a God who knows everything and does as He pleases bother to listen to one of his children? Why would a holy God put up with our unholy tantrums during difficult times in our lives?

A father who squelches expression either through abusive anger or passive detachment teaches his children that expression to God in prayer is equally futile. If these children do ever express themselves to God, they believe that they must be guarded and refined in what they say.

A man who was not listened to by his father will also tend not to listen to God in prayer. Prayer to him is not a dynamic two-way conversation but a talking into the air to a non-listening God without quietly listening to his heavenly Father's voice. He has learned that God doesn't listen to his prayers and he doesn't need to listen to God. The result of these lies planted by the enemy is lifeless prayer.

My wife and I used to take in foster babies, many of whom had previously been in a group home. When the baby cried, the group foster parent did not respond, listen to the child as he or she really needed to be listened to. When these children came to us, we noticed that for a while they would not cry. That was not because they were in superior emotional health but rather, much to the contrary, they had learned that no one was there to listen or respond to them as they cried. Many men today have been programmed not to cry out to God because they truly believe He is not responsive to their cries.

It is amazing when we look at the lives of Abraham, Moses , Job, and David how God listened and accommodated Himself to these men. In Moses' case God listens and responds to Moses' plea that the Israelites be saved from destruction. With Abraham, he listens as Abraham keeps coming back to him and asking him to lower the number of righteous people he would need in order to spare the city of Sodom. And how amazing that God would listen to the raw rantings of Job and David who were in deep pain and cried out to God through their writings. He did not condemn but He honored them by listening to them, giving them the opportunity to express themselves fully to Him.

Our own view of God may have been shaped by our fathers who did not listen to us very well. We heal from this by choosing to turn from this generational sin and begin listening to our children. By doing this we are laying a solid spiritual foundation in our children's lives while at the same time coming to know increasingly the heart of Another Father. This Father gave the life of His eternal Son so that He would be able to listen and respond to us, his blood-bought children.

What the Scriptures Have to Say about Active Listening

Admittedly, there are no direct commands that tell fathers to listen to their children. But there are many admonitions to God's people that can be easily applied to fathers and their children.

Solomon is believed to have authored the major portion of the book of Proverbs. He is widely regarded as the wisest man who has ever lived. His book is largely made up of words of wisdom from a father to his son.

> *"The way of a fool seems right to him, but a wise man listens to advice."*
>
> (Proverbs 12:15 NIV)

The Bible describes a fool as a person who does not listen to others, one who is not teachable. If, as a father, you do not model a listening attitude to your children, you model foolishness. It is no wonder that a man who does not listen to his children when they are young finds that they do not listen to him when they grow older.

"Better a patient man than a warrior, a man who controls his temper than one who takes a city."
(Proverbs 16:32 NIV)

I have a little sign in my office that reads, "MY WIFE SAYS I DON'T LISTEN TO HER. At least I think that's what I think she said." It is kind of cute but there is truth to that saying. Why? Could it be the impatient bottom-line attitude we men often adopt? We men can easily assume a default position of raising our voices in irritable anger rather than seeking to understand. Solomon writes that a man who is calm and self-controlled in his own home is to be honored above a man who is a conquering warrior of an entire city. It is because a patient, listening husband/father creates the atmosphere for the emotional life of his entire family to grow and blossom. His impact will be both eternal and multi-generational.

"A fool finds no pleasure in understanding, but delights in airing his own opinions."
(Proverbs 18:2 NIV)

Again, not to listen is poor father modeling. Children instinctively ask themselves, "Where does my father really find life? What really motivates him; what drives him?" If they see that we are all about telling others what we think and that we take no joy in understanding others, they will tend to grow up to do the same-even if that very behavior wounded them.

It is all too common today to see adolescents totally self-absorbed. Part of this is the challenge of this stage of life, adjusting to the many changes of adolescence. But I wonder if part of this obsessive self-focus stems from the fact that no one has listened to them. They have seen their fathers model only the desire to be heard. So as they are growing into adulthood they naturally focus their energies on being understood by others rather than in listening and understanding. Like father, like son. The curse is perpetuated.

"He who answers before listening—that is his folly and his shame"
(Proverbs 18:13 NIV).

When our youngest daughter was about ten she started a little habit when I would be talking to her. I would begin to say something to her and in the middle of my sentence she would say, "I know, Dad. You don't have to say it. I know what you are going to say already." The funny thing is that when I would go ahead and ask her to tell me what she thought I was going to say that more often than not it was totally different from what I was going to say. This really bothered me about her until I realized that I had modeled and taught this to her. I was now experiencing what it felt like to have this kind of non-listening behavior thrown right back in my face. It woke me up. Since then I have worked on not doing this to others. It is really a disrespectful thing to do. Essentially it tells the other person, "Don't waste my time. You are so predictable. I will save us both the trouble by saying succinctly what you would take much longer to say because of your lack of eloquence. I am not interested in you expressing yourself. Let me do it for you." How dishonoring to another person, especially to one of our children.

A former pastor of mine used to say repeatedly, "Impression without expression can lead to depression." If that is true then there is no wonder that there is such an increase in depression today especially among the youth. A component of that depression could well be that there is such an overload of impressions children contend with but a lack of opportunities for meaningful expressions to caring fathers. That is something to think about.

"The purposes of a man's heart are deep waters, but a man of understanding draws them out"
(Proverbs 20:5 NIV).

Listening sometimes can be like reaching into a well with an empty bucket to patiently draw up to the surface from the depths below the cool, pure water. This is work and it takes time. I recall a night when one of my sons was very glum at the dinner table. My first reaction was to be annoyed and demand that he "shape up or ship out." But I was able to catch myself on this particular night and said a silent prayer to the heavenly Father to help me be the father my son needed that night.

The rest of the family left the dinner table and I began by asking him what was wrong. His answer was the typical, "Nothing." But his body language betrayed him. His facial expression, his eyes, the way he held his head all said, "plenty is wrong!" It took me about an hour that night to draw my son out and get to the bottom of what was bothering him. He had become caught up in gossip with his friends and it was coming back to bite him. He was convinced that his reputation as an 8th grader was now ruined and for the rest of his junior high and high school years he would be branded as a "gossip."

I was reminded that I had gone through a very similar thing in 8th grade. I did not turn to my father but allowed it to turn into deep depression and self-hatred. But now I could help my son, through listening and empathizing with him. I had to get him to see that the situation he was in was not hopeless. We talked through a plan whereby he could go to those whom he had spoken against and apologize to them. We were able to shift from being overwhelmed by the problem to solving the problem. I encouraged him by telling him that he was doing the courageous thing, the right thing, and that he would feel better with every step he took in the process. We prayed together, asking the heavenly Father for forgiveness. I encouraged him that eventually he would regain a good reputation but also reminded him it would take time, that he needed to be patient and start now by doing the right thing now going to each he had offended and apologizing.

I share this story not so I can boast about my fathering abilities (because, sadly, I have missed opportunities such as these as well) but to demonstrate that in every area of pain we have experienced as sons, we can now find healing by looking to Another Father, our heavenly Father. Then we can do for our sons what we may have needed our fathers to do for us when we were in a similar situation. There is healing available from the heavenly Father if we will just hand Him the natural opportunities our children provide us as they struggle to grow up.

A father keeps tabs on his "sheep," his children, by listening, and by giving careful attention to them. Listening to their children is the only way fathers are able to keep connected to what is going on within their ever-changing worlds. By sowing a listening spirit, fathers reap a deep and satisfying relationship. Using the shepherd-sheep/goat metaphor, Solomon reminds us that after we have been attentive to the needs of our flock, "the lambs will provide you with clothing, the goats with the price of a field. You will have plenty of goat's milk to feed you" (Proverbs 27:26-27a NIV). In other words, listening will boomerang back to bless us!

Three Key Listening Principles

The first principle is "In relating with my children fast is slow, and slow is fast."

It is found originally in the Bible and has been articulated recently by author Steven Covey. James says it like this, "My dear brothers, take note of this: Everyone should be quick to listen, slow to speak, and slow to become angry, for man's anger does not bring about the righteous life God desires" (James 1:19-20 NIV).

By the time I was thirteen years old I had become a lonely, depressed, and angry boy who looked for ways to face my situation. One day my parents caught me with a bag of marijuana hidden in my room. My father, upon finding out, became as angry as I had ever seen him to that point in my young life. He did succeed in putting the fear of God in me and that day he was "God" to me! I quit "cold turkey." But that day left some scars. I realized that I had deeply disappointed him and felt that he was disgusted with me and that he did not like me. I did not like myself either. But I just stuffed the whole experience and moved on. It was many years later that I realized that this incident was part of unexpressed anger toward my father and myself that had turned inwardly to bitterness and later to depression.

I do not blame my father for what he did that day. Being "scared straight" is probably what kept me from continuing down the self-destructive path I was on. But I know that besides feeling the brunt of his justified anger, I also needed a listening, compassionate ear. I am ashamed to say that I have done similar things with my children. Like father, like son. I have just wanted their behavior to change, skipping over the difficult work of seeking to understand their heart struggles. But I am determined in God's strength to listen to my kids and grandchildren. If they disappoint me, I will, in God's strength, remind myself that though they may need me to challenge their behavior, they more importantly need my compassionate heart and listening ear.

This second principle is this: "when listening to my child, small is big and big is small."

To reinforce this, Jesus told His disciples, "See that you do not look down on [see as insignificant] one of these little ones. For I tell you that their angels in heaven always see the face of my Father in heaven" (Matthew 18:10 NIV). Here Jesus is explaining to the disciples that the seemingly small concerns of little children are big concerns to the heavenly Father, so much so that He has powerful unseen angelic beings assigned to their care, regularly reporting to Him on their behalf.

Children have a different sense of what is important than we do. When Sen. John Edwards, the 2004 vice-presidential nominee for the Democratic Party, called home to inform his family that he had just been selected to serve on his Party's presidential ticket, his four-year-old got on the line and responded with something like this, "That's great, Dad, you know what else, I can swim now without my floaties."

And speaking of politics, I happen to be a political junkie. It was during the 2000 vice-presidential debate that I found myself glued to the tube. My daughter Holly was eight years old at that time and she collected Barbie dolls.

Right in the middle of the televised debate, Holly came out and asked me if she could show me her Barbie dolls. Being the practical guy that I am, I thought to myself, "How long could this take, one or two minutes?" So I walked into her room and I saw how they were all neatly lined up. And each Barbie had a story related to her... a very, very long story. You get the picture.

When I realized that this was going to take more time than I had bargained for I decided to cut the "Barbie Show" short by saying to her, "They are great, Holly. Thanks for showing me your Barbies." As I stood up thinking I had pulled off faking being interested in what she had to say, she said in a voice that told me that she had seen right through me, "Dad, you didn't let me show you my Barbies."

That night I failed at listening. That opportunity did not come again to me. I made the mistake of not realizing that what was small to me (her Barbies) was big to her and what was big to me (the vice-presidential debates) was small to her. The things in our lives when we are children that are big to us are understandably small to parents. But parents usually do not slow down and put themselves in the children's shoes. Of course, there are times we need to tell our children to wait, but that is a different issue.

The third principle is this: in a world where everyone is concerned about their own interests, being a listening father is not an obligation, but an opportunity.

The apostle Paul wrote to the Philippians, "Do nothing out of selfish ambition or vain conceit, but in humility consider others better than yourselves. Each of you should look not only to your own interests but also to the interests of others" (Philippians 2:3-4 NIV).

How is listening an opportunity? It is estimated that a child will ask up to 500,000 questions before he/she reaches the age of 15. And I think they ask about 499,995 of those during that one year that they are three years old. But each question is an opportunity to listen. Each question is an opportunity for you to be the one person to give answers that will help your children on their life journeys.

In his letter to the church in Philippi, Paul commended Timothy for his listening heart when he wrote, "I have no one else like him who takes a genuine interest in your welfare. For everyone looks out for his own interests, not those of Jesus Christ" (Philippians 2:19-20 NIV). Men, who else will really listen to our children if not us?

What Researchers Say about Listening

Research has shown that listening is a key component for being an effective father. A study done by the National Center For Fathering revealed that "effective" fathers scored eighty-two percent on their verbal interaction (which included listening) while typical fathers scored an average of sixty-eight percent on the same test.

The National Center For Fathering also discovered that there is a direct correlation between a father who scores high in his listening skills and his motivation. In other words, dads who listen to their children get the most satisfaction in their fathering role.

This begs the question, "What influences what?" "Does listening increase motivation or does increased motivation improve listening? The answer is most likely that this works both ways. A father who is highly motivated will likely want to listen to get to know his children and as he listens and tunes into his children he becomes more motivated.

Paul Tournier, a noted psychologist and theologian, believed it is impossible to overemphasize the immense need humans share to be really listened to, to be taken seriously, to be understood. He taught that no person can develop freely in this world and find life without feeling understood by at least one other individual.

Christian author Ross Campbell has written that truly listening is the giving of a child our full, undivided attention in such a way that he feels without doubt that he is completely loved.

Both research and these experts agree that children need to be listened to in order to reach their full potential.

Why Our Fathers May Not Have Listened Well

The vast majority of sons grew up not being listened to by their fathers. These fathers, even those who had the best of intentions, did not give proper attention to their children's voices. Then, when these children became adults and parents themselves, they came to realize firsthand some of the challenges to listening that their fathers encountered, such as fatigue, impatience, preoccupation with work, marital discord, and anger.

Their fathers usually took on the role of primary and, often, sole provider for the family. That pressure alone was tremendous. The burdens of the job would often be carried home. Many sons have memories of their fathers coming home just trying to unwind and just wanting to be left alone. Their energy had been spent outside the home and they were looking to simply somehow "recharge" after a particularly draining day at work.

For many fathers in that situation, having a child who wants to be listened to is a dreary obligation, not a welcomed opportunity. From the tired father's perspective, the goal of the conversation is for the child to "get to the point," rather than to allow his child an opportunity for expression and for him to gain a greater insight into his son or daughter's heart. Worse yet, some fathers can carelessly belittle or ridicule their child in an effort just to facilitate closure to the conversation. Remember, as my former pastor would say, "impression without expression can lead to depression." Children can become depressed adolescents and adults when the one person they long to have listen to them, their father, does not provide them with that gift of listening.

As I reflected on my family heritage I remembered that my grandfather was one of ten children. I had known this before, but now I see this fact in a different light. With that background and modeling from his father, he probably could not even conceive that a father's job description included listening to his children and he probably did not listen much to his sons.

Generally for fathers of past generations there was very little expectation for them to connect emotionally with their children. This was seen as the job of mothers. There was a division of labor; the father took care of providing the tangibles, the physical things for the home, and the mother took care of the intangibles, those things that make a house into a loving home. It is also safe to say that there existed in past generations a general lack of an accurate understanding of how very important it is for parents to listen to their children.

Why WE Have a Hard Time Listening

The challenge facing fathers at the beginning of the 21st century is all of the above plus some unique elements that no other generation of fathers has faced before. It is as if a supernatural being has masterminded a strategy to prevent fathers from listening to their children. Of course if you are a believer in the Bible, you know that there is such a being, one known as the "god of this world," the devil himself, whose purpose on earth it is to blind the minds of men and women from the glorious gospel of Christ (2 Corinthians 4:4).

One thing that fathers today deal with that our fathers did not have to deal with is the unprecedented explosion of media and information. There is a bombardment of messages that come nonstop through various media, which now includes the Internet. As human beings we cope with this by developing a strong mental screening mechanism, so that we only hear what we deem absolutely necessary to hear. Unfortunately, in this attempt to preserve our sanity, we fathers often inadvertently screen out our children's (and our wife's!) voices as well. It is the proverbial "throwing out the baby with the bath water" phenomenon.

Another new advancement of technology that has had an adverse effect upon fathers' ability to listen to their children is the cell phone. One of the saddest things for me to see is when I observe two people out in public together and one person has a phone glued to his ear—especially when it is a father with his child. This is even more tragic when we realize how the cell phone has invaded the sanctity of family time. When I was in leadership at a former church, I underwent a crisis in which I found it necessary to talk on the cell phone for long periods of time. Even when picking up my kids after school or some other event, I only half-listened to them about their day while in my other ear I dealt with the latest chapter of the crisis.

That is precious time that will never be recovered. After that crisis was past I vowed not to talk on the cell phone while I was in the car or doing something with my children. When we do this we tell our children, or anyone else for that matter, that the person who has called us on the phone has priority for us to listen to right now, even though that person could be thousands of miles away. What a hurtful message to send to those whom we love the most.

Today there are an increasing number of children who have personal cell phones and their own televisions and computers in their rooms. They are consuming the media voraciously and they talk to peers via instant messaging and text messaging, but are they really being listened to by anyone who cares about them? Combine all of this with the disappearance of the family mealtime, and fathers today are taking listening to their children to a new low. But there is hope. Let's first consider some possibilities to proactively choose to become active listeners to our family members.

How Fathers Can Better Listen to Their Kids

No matter where you are in this area or listening, you have room for improvement. The following points are from Dr. Ken Canfield's, "Seven Secrets For Effective Fathers," from a piece entitled, "Turn Down The Noise!."1

*Remove distractions –Turn off the TV, music, or whatever is making noise in the family. If you don't your children will erroneously conclude that they are less important. Remember my cell-phone usage during that church crisis? Too many times we see men make vain attempts to listen while watching TV and without even looking at their child. The message communicated is that what is on that tube is far more interesting than the child is.

*Block out the demanding voices of your schedule – Certainly you have been with some-one who made you feel that they were rushed and that you needed to talk quickly before they hurried off. When I was in college I knew a professor who was so very busy that he would run by and ask how I was doing. And I would sarcastically say, as only a wiseacre college student can say, that my mother had cancer and I had been contemplating suicide. Invariably he would smile as he rushed by and say "Great!"

*Turn a deaf ear to your own prejudged perceptions - The purpose of listening is to gain understanding. Critical analysis can come later. Remember how my then ten-year-old daughter would hold up her hand and say, "Hold it! I know what you are going to say"? Remember how irritated I was until I realized that she learned that from me?

*Do not prepare and deliver your intended speech while your child is talking. I love watching political debate on Fox News.. Even though there is great debate from the left and right of the political spectrum, it is probably the worst training ground for listening to my children. Each guest is thinking about what he will say while his opponent talks. They talk right past each other. Dad, you cannot do that with your kids.

Next time you are trying to listen to one of your children try this:
   Put yourself on your child's level
   Adopt an open posture
   Face your child squarely
   Maintain good eye contact
   Stay relaxed as you listen
   Watch your child's nonverbal behavior
   Give your child positive nonverbal feedback
   Restate back what is said in your own words.

Remember that it is not easy for fathers to listen. Many fathers did not have this modeled for them by their fathers. There are also many distractions. Yet most fathers remember that they longed to be listened to. You can be for your children what you longed for your father to be for you. Listening does not come naturally, but will come only from conscious choices. When you listen to your children you show them real love. You tell them that they are important. You declare that you value what they have to say. What they have to say is the expression of who they really are. So let's listen!

A Father's Prayer of Transformation

Dear Father,

I praise You that with all of Your infinite wisdom, knowledge and understanding You still stoop to listen to each of your sons and daughters. I love You for being a God who repeatedly invites Your children to come to You boldly and confidently in prayer through Your Son, Jesus (Ephesians 3:12). I praise You that You listen to me and truly empathize with me and truly hear my heart and are moved by what concerns me (Hebrews 4:14-16), and that You give grace and help in my time of need.

But Father, I confess that often I don't believe that You really do listen to my prayers. They seem to disappear into space as I pray. I have a hard time believing that You listen to my concerns. Of what significance are they, I think, with all that You are dealing with? Yet I know that I have allowed my human feelings and reasoning to overshadow what You have revealed about Yourself through Your Word (I Corinthians 2:4).

I also confess to You that I don't listen well to my wife or my children. I am more concerned with being understood by them than in understanding them. I want to be more concerned for their welfare (Philippians 2:3-4). For this I ask for Your forgiveness and strength to change to become more like You, my Father.

Thank You, dear Lord, for my children and the opportunity that being a father provides me to learn to listen to them as You listen to me. What dignity You bestow on me by listening to me. Father, help me to extend that same honor to my children. Teach me to really attentively listen and seek to understand their hearts (James 1:19-20.) For I know that in so doing I am reflecting Your listening heart and laying a solid foundation in their understanding of Your merciful and gracious character (Matthew 7:24-25).

In the name of Jesus my perfect High Priest, Amen.

Chapter 9

CULTIVATING AWARENESS

"I am the good shepherd; I know my sheep and my sheep know me-just as the Father knows me and I know the Father-and I lay down my life for the sheep."

(John 10:14-15)

The Awareness Lack and Distorted Heavenly Father Images

When children grow up with a father who does not seem to care about their lives, they feel devalued. They may see their father keeping tabs on the city's favorite sports team, the stock market, or the latest political contest, and it seems their father is far less interested in knowing about the ins and outs of their own seemingly insignificant life.

When children begin to picture God and hear about His omniscience, that He knows everything about everything, they may believe it on a cold matter of fact intellectual level but not on the heartfelt emotional level. When a crisis hits and they think of God, they will tend to picture a God who is not paying full attention, who allowed something bad to happen to them because He did not know, or did not care to know, all the facts. Prayer for them is not affirming to their Father what He already knows intimately but informing an out-of-touch God of the facts that He is unaware of or is unconcerned about. In this hard soil of feeling neglectfully unknown, a trusting faith has a hard time taking root!

Let's take a peek at a scene that is not all that uncommon in America today. The following true story I first heard in Dr. Ken Canfield's, "Seven Secrets Of Effective Fathers" seminar:

"Robert grew up in a small Midwestern town where the high school football team had a special tradition. Before the seniors played their final home game, each boy's father would get to take the microphone and announce his son's name, number, and position over the P.A. system. It was a tradition. As you might guess, each of those boys looked forward to that moment from the time they were tossing the football on the elementary school playground. You know that they were thinking: 'Some day my dad is going to come out here and say my name and my number and my position.'

Robert wasn't very big or extremely quick, so he played on the second string, but he loved the game of football and enjoyed the chance to play. Well, the last game rolled around and Robert stood on the field as the microphone was passed down the row. Finally, it was his father's turn. 'Well," his dad said a little hesitantly, "my son's name is Robby Harmon and his number is twenty-two and he plays (pause), well, I think he plays halfback." He laughed nervously, and tense giggles were heard from the people in the stands.

But out on the field, number twenty-two felt as if someone had just stuck a knife in his heart. It seemed to him that his father had little idea about who he was or the dreams and desires that were important to him. Even today, fifty years later, Robert can't tell this story without a lump swelling in his throat and a tear coming to his eye."

When you read Robert's story you might feel a sense of sadness. You know that something is clearly not right there. Probably there was no other person in the entire world that Robert wanted to know him and be proud of him as much as his dad. And why is that? Why do sons (and daughters) place the burden on their fathers to be known by them? Why do we all long that Dad knows our hopes, our dreams, our hurts and pains? Why do we care?

The Longing for Every Child To Be Known

Every person is a human being what is made in the image of God and has a built in two-fold desire at the deepest level to know Him and be known by Him. Those of us who believe in a personal God especially desire that the One who made us also knows us and cares about us.

In the natural realm, the father is the "creator" (small c) of his children, the one who plants the seed of life by impregnating the mother. He determines your gender, your DNA, your very identity. Your earthly father is the closest picture that you have of the Creator God. Taking nothing away from the equal glory and wonder of women, you know that they would not be able to give birth without the contribution of a man's sperm. Today it is true that with artificial insemination and sperm banks, both of which have sought to de-emphasize the father's importance in a child's life, the children produced in this way still have shown a great longing to know their fathers and perhaps better know themselves.

The Scriptures reveal God as Father, Son, and Holy Spirit. A father takes on the very name that God the heavenly Father has for Himself. "For this reason I kneel before the Father from whom His whole family in heaven and earth derives its name." (Ephesians 3:14 NIV). What dignity has been bestowed upon fathers as they have been given the very title that has been derived from the Father God Himself!

So every child, deep within his soul, at the very depth of his spirit, even below the conscious level, yearns to know and be known by his Creator. A father represents the closest earthly, visible connection to fulfilling that longing.

A father also signifies his value to his children. The father is the first outsider to welcome them into the world. A mother is physically joined to her child by an umbilical cord. They have shared life together for nine months and then will continue to bond through nurturing, protecting, comforting, and feeding after birth.

But it is the father, an "other," who really chooses to embrace and value his child by welcoming him into the world. I am the third child of four and the only son in my family. My parents had my two older sisters right after WW II. During the Korean War, my father, who was then in the Marine Corps Reserves, was called up as bomber pilot and was separated from the family for nearly a year. His plane was shot down, but fortunately for me (and my younger sister yet to be born) he landed safely in the water near a friendly base and was soon rescued by helicopter. My mother became pregnant with me soon after his return.

So there was this six-year gap between my sister Lynda and myself. After those six years of having two girls, I believe my parents were ready for a son. Back then people actually had to wait for the birth to know the child's gender. So when I arrived my father was so excited that he walked around the neighborhood handing out cigars. You know, somehow, I never get tired of hearing that story!

Why did I love to hear that story more than anything else that my mother would tell me about how *she* felt at my birth? There was something in me that desired to be welcomed, to be well thought of, and to be known by my father. To me, his welcoming me into this world told me that I was significant and of value. I will always love my mother, but it was my father and my father's attention I craved. The fact that he knows me and thinks about me was and still is very important to me. And any effort on my father's part to enter into my world is like a mirror reflecting my worth and value back to me.

Far too many sons enter the world today with this mirror shattered. It is no wonder they grow up angry and hungry to find any possible avenue, legitimate or not, that will allow them to enjoy some feeling of importance.

A father's knowing love mirrors to a child what every child longs for even if he does not realize it. Every child wants to be wanted, chosen, and thought of as special. The Bible says that it is God the Father who chooses each of us as His sons and daughters. But it took the sacrifice of His Son to make such a relationship with Him a reality.

A father reflects God the Father to his child because he chooses to love his child in a way that is different than a mother's love. His choice to enter into that child's life is more by sacrificial choice and less by nurturing instinct. A father needs to consciously learn about his children while mothers seem to understand them more naturally. This does not diminish a father's dignity at all.

Sons desire to be chosen, to be claimed, to be valued and known by their fathers. But many have been deeply disappointed. For many sons the disappointment has been devastating. For others the wound has not been as deep. But for nearly every son there exists some measure of innate emptiness, loneliness, some sense of being missed, of being unknown by their fathers.

Why Fathers Today Do Not Know Their Sons

Given the most ideal of circumstances, a father is never adequate to meet that deep ache, that longing to be known by his son. The reason is simply that fathers, born with sinful natures, produce sons who also have self-centered, sinful natures. When this sin nature is combined with the fact that these same sons are made in God's image, there is created a longing planted within for more that any earthly relationship could ever possibly deliver in the best of circumstances. In other words, a son's created dignity creates within him a longing that his own and his father's fallenness could never possibly fulfill in this life.

So for generations fathers and sons have had a difficulty connecting. But today at the beginning of the 21st century, it is a time when fathers are more at risk of not knowing their children than perhaps any other time in history. What is happening today, as previously mentioned, is the result of an ingenious strategy by "the god of this world" to blind the minds of men and women (2 Corinthians 4:4) to the heavenly Father. One of the most effective measures being employed is the breaking of the father-child bond, particularly the father-son bond.

During the Industrial Revolution, for the first time since the days of hunting and gathering men left their homes to go to work. Before that time, during the Agrarian Age, most men almost always worked near the home. From then until now, even with the changes brought about by a greater number of women entering the workforce, a kind of contract has been made between husbands and wives. It goes something like this: I, the husband/father, will look out for the big picture and provide for the family. And you, wife/mother, deal with the details of running the home.

This mentality is ingrained in American families because it has been passed down from one generation to the next. Add to this mix the sexual revolution of the 1960s, no-fault divorce, and the extreme elements of the women's movement of the 1970s, and you have a situation in which fathers are not only cut off from their children but the children are left unprotected and unknown by their fathers.

When a couple divorces, the likelihood of a father knowing or being aware of what is going on in his child's life is greatly reduced. And once the father or the mother remarries the chances decrease even further. Furthermore, all of the studies of cohabitation indicate that this poses a greater danger than marriage for the father-child relationship. If the romantic relationship that formed the child does not last, time, distance, guilt, and shame all combine to cause a father to not know much about his child.

If these current realities were not enough to deal with, consider the media explosion of the last decade. Most fathers have email to keep connected with their children while away from home. And cell phones are handy in knowing where kids are at any given moment in time. But other than that, consider how the various media hinder a father from really knowing his children.

When television first came on the American scene, families began to watch programs together rather than sitting around the dinner table talking, playing board games, or reading together. Then several televisions were placed in the typical home. Then cable channels provided different shows for different age group targets, further fragmenting the family with an endless variety of entertainment options. Kids today spend hours in front of the television or computer playing games and/or talking to one another. But a dad who would like to know his children is left out and in the dark.

Today American children are kept extremely busy with sports and various extracurricular activities. The once-sacred family mealtime has become almost nonexistent in many homes. By necessity, mom and daughter may need to go in one direction and dad and son in another. They all grab their food on the run. There is no time for all of them to sit down and leisurely eat together at home to find out what is going on in each other's lives. The joke where I live is that moms call their kids for dinner by yelling at them at the dinner hour, "Come on, kids; get in the car!"

The compulsion for families to get their kids into sports and activities that emphasize fine-tuned narrow performance rather than broad experience is also a threat to a father trying to know his children. The sense of competition with others who are specializing at increasingly younger ages works against a father and child being able to taste a variety of experiences that would promote a greater understanding of who the child might be or could become. The broader number of experiences a child has, the more that child will learn about himself and the more a father can learn about his child.

These are just a few of the factors that work against fathers knowing their children. For a man, this creates a deep pain that he will likely pass on to his children unless he recognizes it and begins to live a lifestyle of repentance, turning from his and his father's sin, and obeying what the Lord would have him do in following Another Father's path.

That Pain That Never Seems to Go Away

In very rare instances, the father of an adult child has an "epiphany" and seeks to know his children when he realizes that he has fallen short. When this occurs, this is wonderful and healing for both father and son. But for the vast majority of fathers and sons the relationship as adults feels like the song written by Barry Manilow, called "Ships." In that song Manilow describes a father and son who are together but are separated by the inability to genuinely connect on an emotional level. Father and son are physically close but they feel the deep ache of being strangers. The pain of not being known by a father usually remains for the rest of the adult father-son relationship. This pain increases over the years as time, aging, and distance do their work and the reality that so much will be left unsaid between father and son sets in. This void was also powerfully portrayed by Mike And The Mechanics in their hit song, "The Living Years."

The "being missed" feeling often happens again when the son becomes a father himself. If he continues the pattern of disconnection as a grandfather, the son feels rejected again. And the missed son will be missed again by his father-turned-grandfather because, instead of being an involved grandpa, he wounds again, now as a detached retired person.

How a Father Can Be More Intentional in Knowing His Child

I have found the following to be helpful in being proactive in knowing my children:

1. **Plan one-on-one time with each child on a regular basis.** I know I have already mentioned this in another chapter, but one-on-one time with our kids is crucial to tuning into their world. In our family we call this "Face Time," and our kids have learned to look forward to this time with dad. As my kids went through their teen years these times sometimes were often quiet, but I have found that the silence often led to real conversations of depth. It doesn't matter where we go. I let them decide where they want to go. It is just "hang time." These are times where I get to know their hearts as I pay attention to what comes out of their mouths. When my kids feel safe they tend to open up, especially when I don't try and push the conversation. As Jesus said, "The things that come out of the mouth come from the heart" (Matthew 15:18 NIV). The goal is not to try to fix our children but to understand them better.

2. **Spend time on your child's turf.** The National Center For Fathering has a program called WatchDOGS. The "DOGS" stands for "Dads Of Great Students." It is an ingeniously simple concept used to get fathers on their kids' school campus for one or two days a year. The impact on both father and child is phenomenal. The reason I believe that this program is so effective is that it taps deeply into the longing of children to

be known by their fathers. The fathers who attend and support their child at school enter into their child's world. That one day spent at school enables him as a father to be able to understand better what his child goes through each day. It helps him to ask better questions and it gives him more empathy when his child is struggling. The dad feels more confident to ask the teacher questions about his child and gains even more understanding.

NOTE: This is just one idea. There are many other ways for a father to get on to his child's turf. I have found that carpooling and just listening to how my kids interact with their friends is very enlightening. As Yogi Berra used to say, "You can observe a lot by watching."

3. **Regularly communicate with your wife about your children.** As already stated, a mother is a gold mine of knowledge or, as I like to say, "the mother lode of fatherhood wisdom." The key is for the father to regularly initiate communication with his wife with the aim of better understanding what is going on with their children. This takes the energy of initiation and the humility to be teachable. My wife and I have tried to make regular communication about our kids a priority in our relationship.

4. **Listen to your child's teachers, coaches, and pastors.** Think about what would motivate a person to want to be a teacher, coach, or pastor. It certainly is not the money! These people generally do what they do because they genuinely care about people and they want to make a difference in the lives of kids. Most of the folks in people-helping professions are honored when parents come to them for insight about their children. Yet often fathers do not think about utilizing these valuable resources as they should. It is an opportunity often missed.

5. **Guard the family meal times.** Family meal times are fast disappearing from the American landscape. I have found that my wife and I need to strive diligently to keep mealtimes a priority. For us it is impossible to have a sit-down meal together every night of the week. But each week we get our calendars out and try to carve out as many family meal times as we can. These are times for a father to catch up with what is going on in his children's lives. I repeatedly emphasize that this is a time to talk, and not a time to let the children leave the table too quickly. You may have something that needs to be talked about as a family or something for which you need to pray. These are key times for a father to tangibly demonstrate to his family that he cares enough to want to know what is going on in each family member's life.

6. **Listen to Another Father for your children.** The father who is a follower of Christ is given an extra resource that cannot be underestimated. He has the heavenly Father Himself indwelling him, through the Holy Spirit giving him the very thoughts of God, "We have not received the spirit of the world, but the Spirit who is from God, that we may understand what God has freely given us" (1 Corinthians 2:12 NIV). "For you did not receive a spirit that makes you a slave again to fear, but you have received the Spirit of Sonship and by him we cry, 'Abba, Father'" (Romans 8:15 NIV).

I have found that this Spirit of Another Father has enabled me to pray with a confidence for specific things for my children that I would not have were I depending upon only what I can observe in them. The Father has given me insights into each of my children's destiny that I can cling to in prayer and remind them of when appropriate. It is that picturing of a better future for them that can impart hope, vision, and perseverance to them.

It is hard to explain, but I simply "know" things about each of my children and their destinies. My wife and I have Scriptures for each of them that we hold on to. I confess that my natural human tendency is towards pessimism, so the fact that these promises are hopeful and positive gives me the strong confidence that I am indeed hearing the voice of Another Father. That is why it is vital for every father to spend time in God's Word, listening to His voice on behalf of his children.

How A Father Benefits From Knowing His Child

The first reason should be obvious. Knowing my child is the best way for me to know how to love my child. Many sons have come to realize after years of emotional pain that their dads really did love them. The only problem was the fathers never knew their children enough, so they didn't know how to love them. They both missed out on a lot.

If an archer is ten feet from the target when he aims his arrow, he will probably hit the bull's eye most of the time. But take that same archer, with noble intentions, focus, and motivation and put him 100 yards from the target. That same archer will be lucky to hit the bale of hay holding the target, let alone the target itself. The principle here is: "accuracy decreases with distance." This applies to those fathers who really do love their children but who do not take the time to know them. They will miss hitting the target of the heart most of the time. Investing the effort required to know your children is not fathering harder, but fathering smarter.

King Solomon spoke to shepherds in his book of Proverbs, but he could have just as easily have been speaking to fathers. He said, "Be sure you know the condition of your flocks, give careful attention to your herds; for riches do not endure forever and a crown is not secure for all generations" (Proverbs 27:23-24 NIV). He then goes on to explain that a shepherd who takes care of his animals will have animals that in turn provide for him and his family. It is a wise father who makes the effort to know his children. The blessing he bestows upon them will be multiplied back to him.

The father who knows his children is also a more confident and motivated father. He is like the person who drives down the freeway with his eyes constantly roving over the road ahead, in the rear-view mirror, over to the side mirrors and back to the front again. This is called scanning. He is aware at all times where his car is in the context of the overall flow of traffic. In the same way a father who "scans" sees his child in context and not in isolation. He has a clear perspective of how the child is doing in relationship to a variety of factors. When the child does something good or bad, this father seeks to see it in context. This way he will not under react or over correct.

I have found that my wife is a particularly helpful resource for me in this area. After talking to her, I am usually able to respond more calmly to any given situation with my kids. Listen to the confidence of Jesus when He says, "I am the Good Shepherd. I know My sheep and My sheep know Me, just as the Father knows Me and I know the Father, and I lay down My life for the sheep" (John 10:14-15 NIV).

How A Child Benefits From Being Known By His Father

As knowledge of his children produces confidence in a father, it also produces security in his children. The Lord Jesus Christ models this concept by the way He knows and leads His spiritual children. He says, "My sheep listen to My voice. I know them and they follow Me. I give them eternal life and they shall never perish, no one can snatch them out of My hand. My Father who has given them to Me, is greater than all, no one can snatch them out of My Father's hand. I and the Father are one" (John 10:27-29 NIV).

The relationship between a child knowing that his father knows him and that child's security should be fairly obvious. The Lord Jesus emphases this truth by pointing to the Father's knowledge of His children, "So do not worry saying, 'What shall we eat?' or 'What shall we drink?' or 'What shall we wear?' For the pagans run after these things and your Heavenly Father knows that you need them" (Matthew 6:31-32 NIV).

The issue comes down to trust. A father who makes the effort to really know his children will earn their trust. Simply by changing a couple of words in the following passage it can be applied to a child's relationship with his father: "If (a child) says 'I love God, yet hates his [father] he is a liar, for anyone who does not love his [father] whom he has seen, cannot love God whom he has not seen" (1John 4:20 NIV parenthetic statements added). Though this verse is referring to the love of followers of Christ, there is another principle being taught here. Children are greatly helped in the process of transferring trust to an unseen heavenly Father who knows them perfectly when they have experienced a seen father who seeks to know them imperfectly.

Children are concrete thinkers. As fathers, it is our privilege to be stepping stones for them to use to grow in trusting the all-knowing, all-loving Heavenly Father by showing Him and His Son, Jesus, to them in tangible ways.

Jesus, speaking to His disciples, said, "See that you do not look down on one of these little ones. For I tell you that their angels in heaven always see the face of My Father in heaven" (Matthew 18:10 NIV). The idea of "looking down on" here carries the idea of seeing someone as insignificant. If we see our children as insignificant, somehow not worthy to be known as the glorious people that they are, we do not reflect the heavenly Father's heart for them this "Father in heaven (who) is not willing that any of these little ones should be lost" (Matthew 18:11 NIV).

A Father's Prayer of Transformation

Dear Father,

I praise You that You are a Shepherd who knows His sheep. Your dear Son laid down His life for us, His helpless sheep, knowing our sinfulness and that it would cost Him to be separated from You on that cross and taste hell for every one of us (John 10:14-15). I am amazed that You are aware of when one sparrow falls to the ground. How much more I should trust Your awareness of what goes on in my life (Matthew 10:29-31). I praise You that You are familiar with all of my ways and that familiarity has not bred contempt in You toward me but only more love. Thank You for caring to know about the small things as well as the big things in my world.

But Father, I confess to You that in my heart I often don't feel that You are really aware of the details in my life. When things occur in my life that don't make sense to me or when I don't see You working in the ways I think you should, I begin to feel that You are not aware of my life's details, or that You don't care. I know in my head this isn't true, but my heart says something else (Matthew 6:31-33).

I confess that as a father I have allowed myself to become more aware of things that are not as important as knowing about what is going on in my children's world. In eternity these other things won't matter as much as my awareness of their lives. Forgive me, Father, for this sin of omission and make me a man who will know "the condition of my flocks and give careful attention to my herds," beginning with my own family (Proverbs 27:23).

In the name of Jesus my Shepherd who knows me perfectly,

Amen.

Chapter 10

SHOWING AFFECTION

" For you know that we dealt with each of you as a father deals with his own children, encouraging, comforting and urging you to live lives worthy of God, who calls you into his kingdom and glory"

(I Thessalonians 2:11-12 NIV).

Unloved Sons And Distorted Heavenly Father Images

A child who grows up not feeling loved by his father comes to believe that the words in the Bible about God's love for him are just words.

If a son never hears the words from Dad "I love you," if he never sees his father sacrificially demonstrate his love for him; if he never hears his father say to him in a warm and gentle voice, "Son, I'm proud of you," there will be a disconnect between what he believes in his head and what he believes in his heart , in his experience about God's love.

It is not a stretch to believe that this child will grow up to feel that the love of God is not the kind of love that can be *personally* experienced. He will see God as a person who is quite willing to stand aloof and disconnected from his world. When he sins or fails he will see in his mind's eye a God who is disappointed, distant, and even embarrassed to claim him as His own. Of course the enemy, the forces of darkness, are right there to exploit the situation and add the devil's lies to this sinful deception already occurring.

This is even truer for a child who grows up in a church-attending, Bible-believing family. The danger is particularly acute here because this child will naturally make the earthly father-heavenly Father connection by observing his or her religious father.

With all of this at stake, where do fathers at the beginning of the 21st century stand when it comes to showing affection to their children? To put this question in context, consider what it is like for a child growing up today in America.

Where Is the Love?

It has been said that we live in an age of "emotional asceticism." Just as a desert monk grows accustomed to living on much less physically, we have done this emotionally, learning to expect much less from others—starting in the home. Children growing up in America today have roughly a forty-percent chance that before they turn eighteen years old their biological father will not still be living at home. In the African-American community the percentage is closer to seventy percent. In that context the higher percentage is due more to a high cohabitation and single-parenting rate than a high divorce rate.

Whether divorce or other circumstances cause this absence, the results are the same. Most children suffer the loss of a father's love. Not only does the child lose the father's love but often the loss includes lost "backup love" of an extended family (grandparents, aunts and uncles, etc.) because of the breakup of the family structure.

For many other families a father may be physically present but he is emotionally absent, consumed by his work or some addictive behavior. Mothers today are very likely to be working outside the home – either by economic necessity or by choice for personal fulfillment. Whatever the reasons for this, the results are the same—there is no one left at home to nurture the children on a consistent basis.

This child experiences even more shock to his system when he enters school, the world of wounded peers, teachers, and coaches. More love letdowns. Teachers who are called to really care for their students are often dealing with their own issues. Peers frequently seek to exploit others or use them for their own selfish purposes. Coaches will befriend them if they have talent that will benefit the team and ignore them if they don't. Then there are the pastors, priests and religious figures who are supposed to be safe. A child is growing up today is in a society scarred by sexual scandal among the clergy. Lastly, the media figures that are supposed to be role models are not. They model a hedonistic lifestyle of self-centeredness and, in fact, demonstrate that this lifestyle is handsomely rewarded by society.

The picture is indeed dark. For many kids in America this is becoming reality more often than not and this seems to be increasingly more of a common experience among the youth with each passing year.

How Did We Get Here?

A father's ability to show love to his children today is challenged by a culture obsessed with self-fulfillment and consumed with the pursuit of self-interest at the expense of genuine care for others.

Let's start with a man's own emotional self. By the time a man becomes a husband and father he has learned that true masculinity in our society is demonstrated not by expressing emotions but by suppressing them. The only acceptable masculine displays of emotion seem to be the occasional outbreak of rage and anger or overwhelming joy at an athletic event. Negative feelings are bottled up, and once in awhile, when they cannot be contained any longer, the pressure is often released upon family members in explosive anger.

Unfortunately, this is what many men have learned from their fathers. For those men, their father was driven to prove something to his father through his work effort. He was unable to express love to his children in the home as he had not received father-love himself. This man is now married to a wounded woman who has emotional needs that he is unable to meet. They soon become another classic example of a "two ticks and no dog" marriage where either one person dominates the other or both live a kind of married singleness.

This man could find healing in the presence of other men who would affirm and help him to express love to his family, but he runs from closeness with men for at least two reasons. One is the feeling that building a bond with another man creates uncomfortable same-sex attraction connotations or undercurrents with which he does not want to be associated. But probably the bigger barrier to closeness with other men for a man, if his father has wounded him, is his reluctance to be vulnerable to other men, as these men often trigger painful feelings similar to those he experienced with his father. Watch any sporting event on TV and note how the ads play to this fear. A particular commercial shows men sitting on the couch together, terrified of touching each other. However, once their team scores they are climbing all over each other. Only in that context is it "safe" for men to get close.

The Homeless Male Heroes Of America

John Wayne was a man of action, not talk, when he played a cowboy or soldier in the 1950s and 60s. The 1970s brought us a darker version of the real man in Clint Eastwood's *Dirty Harry*, who was my hero. I remember recently watching a rerun of a *Dirty Harry* movie and as I now saw this guy objectively, I realized that he is really one sick individual. That character certainly was not a man I would now like to emulate but at the time he seemed so cool!

The 1980's gave us Sylvester Stallone's *Rambo* character. And since the 1990s we have had Pierce Brosnan's James Bond character. But these guys aren't home-front heroes, but rather home-less heroes. Each of these men shows his masculinity through cold, steely emotional control, not through any show of warm emotional expression. Notice that we never see these men as committed husbands or caring fathers.

Men are often in a work situation that requires the stifling of emotional response. Generally the work environment stresses rational and emotional control rather than emotional expression. For a large part of his day the typical father is investing into these control tendencies rather than into nurturing behaviors.

These are but some of the key factors that make emotional presence such a challenge for fathers today.

The Importance For Fathers To Show Affection To Their Children

It could be argued that this is just the way we men are. After all, isn't this why God created mothers?

There are two things wrong with this. For one thing an increasing number of women are leaving their nurturing role today for one reason or another. So men are needed more than ever to play at least a part of the nurturing role in their children's lives. In other words, if these children's dads do not nurture them they will not be receiving any emotional encouragement at all.

And the research has repeatedly shown that even children who have nurturing moms greatly benefit when their father also connects emotionally with them.

Let's look at the benefit for girls. It has been demonstrated by surveys that fathers are the first and most important men in girls' lives. It has also been shown that emotionally connected dads provide girls a sense of physical and emotional security. Girls are set up by emotionally distant fathers to look for love in all the wrong places. Simply stated, *fathers are protecting their daughters by connecting with them.*

If boys are not validated and affirmed in their masculinity by their dad in their growing-up years, they become haunted by the fear that they are somehow not man enough. There are many advertisements today that try to goad men into buying products by pandering to this fear.

For those who have studied the underlying causes of same sex attraction, the most reliable predictor has been found to be a lack of emotional bonding with a father or other nurturing male figure. A boy who is emotionally disconnected from his dad is pulled in two directions - either into hyper-masculinity to prove his maleness or into a more feminine identity that will often lead him to a same-sex relationship.

Emotionally distant fathers produce disconnected men who will, in turn, be ill-equipped to nurture their own children. And the beat will go on. Like father, like son, like father, like son, like father, like son…

A Father Can Give Only What He Has First Received

Every human father needs an experiential, vital, living relationship with another father. Ideally, he finds this relationship with the heavenly Father through His Son so that he can become a true vessel of sacrificial love to his family. The Bible teaches that every person who puts faith in Christ becomes a child of the heavenly Father (John 1:12). Sadly, many of those men who are now connected to that Father do not extend that connection to their own fathering. In other words, although they do have Another Father in their life their actual beliefs and behavior are more closely tied to their earthly father. Spiritual growth has to mean that a man's "like father, like son" experience becomes less earthly and more heavenly.

Let's take a look at some biblical examples of men who found Another Father and how the heavenly Father connected with them through touch and words of affirmation.

John the Baptist was the son of Zecharias, a godly Levite priest. The heavenly Father set John apart from birth to be a man filled with the Holy Spirit. His ministry was to turn the Jewish people back to God through repentance; particularly he was to turn the hearts of fathers to their children. And he was to operate in "the spirit and power of Elijah." Elijah was a man who centuries earlier God had anointed to do great miracles. The amazing thing about his ministry was that as great as it was, he anointed another man named Elisha, his spiritual son, to do twice the number of miracles, twenty-eight to fourteen, if we were to keep track of what he did. *The spirit and power of Elijah is the spirit that can enable a man to pass a double blessing on to the next generation.*

The Bible tells us that John, operating in the spirit and power of Elijah, was performing baptisms in the Judean wilderness when he saw his half cousin, Jesus, coming to him to be baptized. We know that Jesus had loved and obeyed His earthly (surrogate) father, Joseph, but He had Another Father, the heavenly Father, whom He had been in relationship with from eternity past. The heavenly Father did two things to show His affection to Jesus, His Son, as Jesus was about to launch His earthly ministry.

He descended upon Jesus through the Holy Spirit in the form of a dove. I imagine this dove gently landing on Jesus' shoulder, feeling like the gentle touch a father would put on a son to reassure and affirm him. Then secondly the Father spoke to His Son and said for all to hear, "You are My Son, whom I love, with You I am well pleased" (Luke 3:22 NIV).

The Bible thus records that before Jesus went into the wilderness for a forty-day period of testing and then into an arduous three-year ministry, He received a gentle touch on the shoulder and a loving, affirming voice from the heavenly Father.

The Model of the Heavenly Father

The Bible also records that shortly before Jesus was to go to the cross and face His greatest test of all, He took three of his disciples up on a mountain. There He became transfigured into a glorious brightness in His face and clothes and Moses and Elijah met with Him. "A bright cloud enveloped them, and a voice from the cloud said, 'This is My Son, whom I love, with Him I am well pleased. Listen to Him" (Matthew 17:5). Here the Father does something very similar, but this time gives His Son a "cloud hug," enveloping Him with a cloud and giving him affirming words.

In one short sentence the Father shows how to love your children. The invisible heavenly Father does something to show His affection. He touches His son, by sending a cloud to envelop Him.

The first thing you can do to show your affection to your children is physical touch. A well-known UCLA study has shown that an adult needs to experience eight to ten physical touches per day to experience full emotional health.[1]

Not many grown men can remember regularly being hugged by their fathers. Not many fathers wrestle with their sons. Not many children are even touched lovingly by their fathers on a regular basis. This is important! My children are getting older now and they won't admit that they need hugs and touches from me but they still do, and I need to remember to do that. The apostle John knew the affirming touch of Jesus probably more than any of the other disciples since we are told he leaned his head against Jesus at their last meal together in the upper room.

The second element we see exhibited here by the heavenly Father is affirming words. The heavenly Father spoke to Jesus' three human needs—for identity, security, and competency.

"This is My Son," reminded Jesus of His identity, that He was His Father's Son. He was somebody very special to His Father. He belonged to the Father in heaven. Your children are important because they belong to you, not because of what they do. They are living extensions of you into the future.

I remember spending a week with my cousin in Los Angeles once. And my uncle said to someone he ran into when we were out and about, "This is my sister's boy." As true as that was my uncle was my mother's brother, I hated to hear that. I longed rather to be known as "my father's boy." I longed for my dad's identity, not my mother's. I was his son and I longed to be known as such.

When the heavenly Father said, "…Whom I love," He spoke to Jesus' need for security. He was loved for who He was, not what He had ever done or was about to do. It is important to also note that the heavenly Father said this to Jesus before He even began His important life work. Not many of us heard our fathers say, "I love you." The fact is few men can recall these words coming from their father. This is a phenomenon that has to stop with you. Your children need to hear from you over and over that you love them. You cannot tell them often enough.

"In Him I am well pleased," addresses Jesus' need to be assured of His competency. Jesus was about to face the temptations of Satan in the wilderness where He would be tempted to translate suffering into thinking His Father was displeased with Him. The heavenly Father reminded Him that He was proud of Him. All children need to know that their father is proud of them before they go out to face the inevitable challenges of life.

Dad, if you don't let your children know how proud you are of them they may spend the rest of their lives trying to prove themselves to you. Your children need to know that you are proud of them and that you are excited about every step of progress they make in their lives. They need to know that you believe in them, that in your eyes they have *already* succeeded and you are confident in their future success. Think of things that you are genuinely proud of in each of your children. Then simply tell them. Write out a list and keep it handy as a reminder, if that helps.

The Bible says that Jesus, at the end of His earthly ministry, spoke often with his spiritual children, His disciples. One of them, named Philip, who had heard from Jesus about the heavenly Father for the past three years, finally said to Jesus, "Lord, show us the Father and that will be enough for us" (John 14:8 NIV).

Jesus explained that all they had seen Him do and heard Him say came from the heavenly Father. But then Jesus said something startling. He said, "I tell you the truth, anyone who has faith in me, will do what I have been doing. He will do even greater things than these, because I am going to the Father"(John 14:12 NIV).

This Father-heart lives in Jesus, Himself the Son of God. The Son's heart is to speak to His Heavenly Father on His sons' (disciples') behalf so that they may do even greater things than He did for the Heavenly Father's glory (John 15:7-9). When the apostle John was an old man, he wrote to his friend Gaius and exclaimed in jubilation, "I have no greater joy than to hear that my children are walking in the truth" (3 John v. 4 NIV).

The Apostle Paul shows the power of affirming words and touch when he reminded his spiritual son, Timothy, of his identity as a son of another Father. He wrote to him in 2 Timothy 1:6-7 NIV, "For this reason I remind you to fan into flame the gift of God, which is in you through the laying on of my hands. For God did not give us a spirit of timidity, but a spirit of power, of love and of self-discipline."

These examples show how these men needed to be loved by Another Father and they needed that love to be affirmed in their lives by another man. Jesus needed the voice and touch of His Father. The Apostle John needed the voice and touch of Jesus. Timothy needed the voice and touch of the Apostle Paul. This is how the reality of Another Father is conveyed to sons so they can pass this onto their sons, both physically and spiritually. A couple of years I found myself saying goodbye to another college freshman in our family-this time my oldest son. After helping him settle into his dorm room we walked out to the car together. "I'm going to miss you,

Son," I said, tearing up and putting my arm around his shoulder. I was startled when his arm reached right back around my shoulder, now at my same height, and replied to me with an even deeper voice than mine, "I'm going to miss you too, Dad." We hugged in the parking lot unashamed of our embrace. I will always treasure that moment.

In summary, a father shows affection to his children from his heart. What he has in his heart will be expressed by touch and through words. But it all starts in the heart. For it is the heart that desires, believes, longs for his child to be blessed more than he himself has been blessed. A father must be willing to do whatever it takes to let his child know his love. That is living in the spirit and power of Elijah. That is the true turning of his heart to his children.

The "Re-Fathering" of a Son

The primary ways for a man to be "re-fathered" are through exercising simple faith in the heavenly Father's words, by actively praying for healing and living out practically the fruits of repentance. Jesus said to His followers in John 14:21 NIV, "Whoever has my commands and obeys them, He is the one who loves Me. And He who loves me, will be loved by my Father, and I too will love him and show Myself to him."

What a promise! If a man chooses to follow Jesus and obey His command to love and serve others, beginning with his own family, this man will come to experientially know the heavenly Father's love. The "how-to's" of this love will be revealed to this man who may have had either poor father modeling or worse yet, no father model at all. But this is not enough. Every father needs the support of other men. That is the way we have been made—to be interdependent upon one another.

When a man chooses to become part of a small group of God-seeking men he provides a chance for the Holy Spirit to "re-father" him. Many men have never had an experience of being re-fathered like this. The Spirit of Sonship is available to every man who comes to the heavenly Father through His Son, Jesus Christ. In a small community of other sons, the Holy Spirit can "re-father" men to become emotionally present, first to one another and then to the members of their own families.

The Apostle Paul reminds us in Romans 8:15 NIV, "For you did not receive a Spirit that makes you a slave again to fear (the fear of intimacy and of vulnerability to others), but you received the Spirit of Sonship and by Him, we cry 'Abba, Father.'" (parenthetic statement added)

It is common for men to say that their small group becomes like a father to them. Author Gordon Dalbey says of this experience, "It makes sense, both theologically and practically." He has seen men healed in the context of relating to each other, but it is also clear that the presence of God's Spirit comes in special ways to men where two or three are gathered in the name of God's Son (Matthew 18:20).

Today, if we men are willing to humble ourselves before other men and submit themselves to this "re-fathering" process, we can powerfully convey to our children the message of the heavenly Father's perfect love. Our children need their fathers' affirming touch, their fathers' words, their fathers' modeling, and their fathers' prayers in concert with those of Jesus Christ before the heavenly Father on their behalf.

A Father's Prayer of Transformation

Dear Father,

I praise You that when You said "This is My Son, whom I love, with Him I am well pleased" (Matthew 3:17, 17:5) You were saying this to me as well because I have been joined to Him eternally through the cross (Galatians 2:20). You have fully accepted me in Him (Ephesians 1:6) and You have poured out the same love upon me as You have for eternity on Your own Son, Jesus (John 15:9, 16:27). I praise You that You have chosen not to love me half-heartedly but rather to lavishly pour Your affection on me through Your Holy Spirit (Romans 5:5, 1 John 3:1-3).

But, Dear Lord, I confess to You that I often don't feel the love and affection that Your Word says that You have for me. I confess that because I don't feel this love that I am walking not by faith but by sight and by my feelings (2 Corinthians 5:7). I often live with a sense of distance from You. I confess that because of this I don't portray to my children a clear picture of Your love. They see such a distorted picture of Your perfect and unconditional love through me!

Thank You for all of the ways that You daily show me Your loving care. I thank You that what Your word says about Your love for me is true despite what my feelings tell me. Will You remind me afresh and open my eyes anew to Your love for me that I can be a vessel of that love for my family? I want to love them from the overflow of Your love for me (1 John 4:16-21). Even my Lord Jesus depended upon Your love for Him in order for Him to be able to love and serve His disciples (John 13:4-6).

In the name of Your Son, Jesus, the Lover of my soul, Amen.

SECTION 4

INTRODUCING YOUR CHILD TO ANOTHER FATHER— MEETING SPIRITUAL NEEDS

For a father to meet his child's physical needs is essential and to meet his children's emotional needs is crucial. But what is the importance of a father meeting his child's spiritual needs? What about the need for a father to introduce his child to Another Father? A father can raise successful, well-adjusted, emotionally healthy children, but if he passes on generational sin and fails to point his child to the heart of the heavenly Father, he has fallen short of the mark. Jesus said it best when He said, "What good is it for a man to gain the whole world, yet forfeit his soul?" (Mark 8:36). Translation for fathers: "What good is it for a father to provide every need his children have—both physical and emotional—and yet fail to provide for his childrens' greatest need, that of coming to know Another Father and possessing a genuine hope that is beyond this brief earthly life?" This is a warning to one who considers himself a Christ-follower as much as for one who does not. Listen to Ken's story.

Ken was a muscular, former college football player with an attractive wife and two beautiful young children. On the outside he looked as though he had it all together. He made the time to become an over-achieving layman at his church. But Ken now confesses, "The reason I was so active is that I was portraying myself as someone I wasn't on the inside but as someone I wanted to be. I did all the right things on the outside."

Inside, Ken was an angry man. He was the son of an angry father who had taught through example to process his emotions by exploding with anger. His father was a wounded man, scarred by his own father who had yelled at him when he was an oversized 13-year-old playing with trucks in the front yard. "When in the hell are you going to grow up?!" Ken's father recalls his father saying this to him just a week before his death. The relationship was never able to be resolved. This anger was passed on down to Ken.

Ken and his wife hit the wall at a marriage conference. His wife had become increasingly frustrated with the anger that he was showing toward her and their young children who had become afraid of him. She finally broke at the conference, "I just can't take it anymore." She also pointed out to him that, in her mind, his obsessive church involvement was an avoidance of dealing with his issues and that the church had become his "mistress."

Right there, Ken was at a fork in his marital road. He could have thrown blame back to his wife and denied the validity of her observations or he could do what he decided to do. He chose to resign from all of his involvement right away and finally take a look at what was going on "under the hood" of his life.

The heavenly Father used this issue of Ken's anger and its destructiveness in his family to get his attention. He began to deal with an issue he may never have addressed without that pressure. That was the goad that prodded him to take a painful look at what he needed to change in his heart.

In Ken's own words, "The effect of having those comments from my wife caused me to say to myself, 'I don't want my kids to be like me. I don't want to pass this baton of anger and whatever else is going on to my kids.'" Shortly after resigning his various responsibilities at church, he entered a desert place in his life that culminated in getting some professional counseling.

Since that time Ken has slowly but surely grown in a new, healthy relationship with his wife and their two children. He and his wife have prayed and seen God answer the prayer to "give back the years the locusts have eaten" (Joel 2:25). Ken knows the power of modeling in his own battles, the multigenerational impact that fathers have on families for good and evil.

He began rebuilding his relationship with his family by being honest and by asking their forgiveness for his wrong behaviors and attitudes. The process continued as his children grew into adulthood. As the Lord reveals new insights to his generational patterns of sin, Ken continues to respond to God with the strong desire to protect his son and daughter from inheriting a generational bondage to the sin of destructive anger.

He did run the risk of seeing himself as a victim and becoming stuck in an attitude of blame. But in Ken's case his heart was turned toward his children and it was their future welfare that became the driving motivation for life change.

As Ken took steady steps of repentance and obedience he came to know that the heavenly Father's love was quite different than any earthly father's love he had ever experienced. He remembers today the quiet unmistakable voice he heard in his heart that said simply, "The issue, Ken, is that you can't accept grace. You don't have to prove yourself. I love you just the way you are. Just let Me love you."

As he sought to model to his children, what would bring life rather than death to them, he became transformed in his relationship with his heavenly Father. He has come to understand the "like father, like son" principle through the anguish of seeing himself live out his father's anger which had begun to be seen in his children's lives. Ken is now courageously setting the pace in his family by modeling humility, reconciling relationships, and sacrificially serving his family..

As we move into our last section, the two chapters, "Modeling Integrity" and "Equipping Spiritually," realize that although these two chapters are *last* they certainly are not *least*!

Chapter 11

MODELING INTEGRITY

"The righteous man leads a blameless life, blessed are his children after him"

(Proverbs 20:7).

Poor Modeling and Distorted Heavenly Father Images

You either had a father who generally "walked his talk" or you had a father who disappointed you in the way his life didn't match his words. You have been influenced in your view of the heavenly Father by your father's example and you influence your children's view of God by what you model. There is much at stake! In a very real sense a hypocritical father teaches his children that the heavenly Father's words are one thing and his actions are another—that he cannot be trusted. That is the opposite of integrity, or a life where man's values are "integrated" into every area of his life.

If a father does not live out his life consistently, he teaches his children that God's Word is hollow. He conveys that God cannot be depended upon by His children. A child will tend to project this experience with his father onto his image of God the Father. When God's promises are not answered according to his timetable he will conclude that God is unreliable, just as his father was. You are asked to consider in this chapter all that is at stake for your children in the area of modeling, of "walking the talk," of consistently showing the way "home" (safely into the heavenly Father's arms) to your children.

Butch and Eddie by: Author Unknown, Source Unknown

World War II produced many heroes. One such man was Butch O'Hare. He was a fighter pilot assigned to an aircraft carrier in the South Pacific.

"One day his entire squadron was sent on a mission. After he was airborne, he looked at his fuel gauge and realized that someone had forgotten to top off his fuel tank. He would not have enough fuel to complete his mission and get back to his ship. His flight leader told him to return to the carrier.

"Reluctantly he dropped out of formation and headed back to the fleet. As he was returning to the mothership, he saw something that turned his blood cold. A squadron of Japanese Zeroes were speeding their way toward the American fleet. The American fighters were gone on a sortie and the fleet was all but defenseless. He couldn't reach his squadron and bring them back in time to save the fleet. Nor could he warn the fleet of the approaching danger.

"There was only one thing to do. He must somehow divert them from the fleet. Laying aside all thoughts of personal safety, he dove into the formation of Japanese planes. Wing-mounted 50-calibers blazed as he charged in, attacking one surprised enemy plane and then another. Butch weaved in and out of the now broken formation and fired at as many planes as possible until finally all his ammunition was spent.

"Undaunted, he continued the assault. He dove at the Zeroes, trying at least to clip off a wing or tail in hopes of damaging as many enemy planes as possible and rendering them unfit to fly. He was desperate to do anything he could to keep them from reaching the American ships. Finally, the exasperated Japanese squadron took off in another direction.

"Deeply relieved, Butch O'Hare and his tattered fighter limped back to the carrier. Upon arrival he reported in and related the event surrounding his return. The film from the camera mounted on his plane told the tale. It showed the extent of Butch's daring attempt to protect his fleet. He was recognized as a hero and given one of the nation's highest military honors.

"And today, O'Hare Airport in Chicago is named in tribute to the courage of this great man.

"Some years earlier there was a man in Chicago called Easy Eddie. At that time, Al Capone virtually owned the city. Capone wasn't famous for anything heroic. His exploits were anything but praiseworthy. He was, however, notorious for enmeshing the city of Chicago in everything from bootlegged booze and prostitution to murder.

"Easy Eddie was Capone's lawyer, and for a good reason. He was very good at what he did. In fact, his skill at legal maneuvering kept Big Al out of jail for a long time. To show his appreciation, Capone paid him very well. Not only was the money big, Eddie got special dividends. For instance, he and his family occupied a fenced-in mansion with live-in help and all of the conveniences of the day. The estate was so large that it filled an entire Chicago city block. Yes,

Eddie lived the high life of the Chicago mob and gave little consideration to the atrocity that went on around him.

"Eddie did have one soft spot, however. He had a son whom he loved dearly. Eddie saw to it that his young son had the best of everything: clothes, cars, and a good education. Nothing was withheld. Price was no object. And, despite his involvement with organized crime, Eddie even tried to teach him right from wrong. Yes, Eddie tried to teach his son to rise above his own sordid life. He wanted him to be a better man than he was. Yet with all his wealth and influence, there were two things that Eddie couldn't give his son, two things that Eddie sacrificed to the Capone mob that he could not pass on to his beloved son: a good name and a good example.

"One day, Easy Eddie reached a difficult decision. Offering his son a good name was far more important than all the riches he could lavish on him. He had to rectify all the wrong that he had done.

"He would go to the authorities and tell the truth about Scar-face Al Capone. He would try to clean up his tarnished name and offer his son some semblance of integrity. To do this he must testify against the Mob, and he knew that the cost would be great. But more than anything, he wanted to be an example to his son. He wanted to do his best to make restoration and hopefully have a good name to leave his son.

"So he testified. Within the year, Easy Eddie's life ended in a blaze of gunfire on a lonely Chicago street. He had given his son the greatest gift he had to offer at the greatest price he would ever pay.

"I know what you're thinking. What do these two stories have to do with one another? Well, you see, Butch O'Hare was Easy Eddie's son."

As we read this story you are no doubt amazed at the power of one father's model of integrity to his son. But of course modeling can go both ways. Harry Chapin's classic song, called "Cat's In The Cradle," in contrast, depicts how a father models misplaced priorities to his son. When this father grows old he finds that his son has learned well just what had been modeled to him. He reaps the poor modeling that he had sown into his son's life.

It is so easy for fathers to model the wrong things like the father in Chapin's famous song rather than modeling the right things as did Easy Eddie to his son Butch. The hard way takes tough conscious choices. The easy way takes only day by day going with the flow. And this poor modeling "by default" is being perpetuated generation after generation. Fathers continue to do the very things to their children that were so hurtful to them when they were children. Like father, like son.

There are a number of temptations that a father faces that keep him from modeling the right things to his children. I have identified three. There are probably more but here are three big ones. The first that comes to mind is a father's *pride*. There is something in us as that not

147

want to humble ourselves before our children to be accountable to them for our actions. Very few men can recall ever hearing an apology from their fathers.

Another temptation facing a father is *lust*. This is a close cousin to pride. The focus of lust is to gratify their desires here and now without any thought about the effects it will have upon his family—his wife, children or grandchildren. This desire is for instant self-gratification.

Then a third temptation that fathers face is in modeling to their children is to fall for the deception that a father's example does not matter. Let's call it *denial*. This temptation is appealing because it seems to offer a type of freedom to a man. But if he is honest he will realize that his father's example greatly impacted him for good and for bad and he knows the same is true for his impact upon his children.

The Father Modeling Hall of Shame

In the Bible there is an unofficial "Father Modeling Hall of Shame." *One father who best illustrates the problem of pride is King Hezekiah.* Now he really wasn't a bad king at all. In fact he was compared to King David in his godliness. It was said of him that "there was no one like him among all the kings of Judah, either before him or after him" (2 kings 18:5 NIV). What a tribute! But Hezekiah developed a pride problem after his life had been spared from a serious illness and he was given another fifteen years to live. In his desire to impress an envoy of Babylonians who came to visit him after he recovered from his illness, he forgot God. Hezekiah wanted to impress his visitors and display to them his wealth. He showed him all that he had in the storehouses. This act of arrogance left Judah later vulnerable to an attack from Babylon (2 Kings 12-21).

Isaiah confronted the king about his careless pride and prophesied that some of Hezekiah's very own children would be carried away into captivity in Babylon. The prophet told Hezekiah that some of them would be made into eunuchs and serve in the palace of the king of Babylon. Hezekiah's response to that was incredible. "The word of the LORD you have spoken is good...for he thought, 'will there not be peace and security in my lifetime?'" (2 Kings 20:19 NIV). This has to be the most selfish comment a father ever uttered. What a warning this is for fathers today. Hezekiah was a good and godly king and yet his selfish pride doomed his children. His son Manasseh became known as Judah's most evil king in its history. He rebuilt the places of idolatry that his father had destroyed. In fact Manasseh was so evil that it was said of him: "Manasseh led them astray, so that they did more evil than the nations the LORD had destroyed before the Israelites" (2 Kings 21:9 NIV).

The father who fell into the trap of lust is Esau. Esau was the twin brother of Jacob. Jacob later was called "Israel" and became the father of the Jewish nation. He was the one who inherited the birthright blessing from his father Isaac. Jacob stole that birthright from Esau through manipulation. He knew Esau's weakness-that he loved to eat. So one day when Esau came in from a tough period of hunting without bagging any game, Jacob manipulated Esau to give him his birthright for a bowl of red stew. Esau agreed and showed through this that he was a man who was willing to sacrifice what was lasting and eternal for instant gratification.

But what happened to Esau's descendants? They became the Edomites. They were a thorn in the side of Israel for hundreds of years. They were lost as far as their relationship with God was concerned. We also know that they disappeared from history around 70 A.D. during the time of the destruction of Jerusalem.

The father who epitomized unbelief is Eli the high priest. He had two sons, Hophni and Phineas, of whom Scripture says, "they had no regard for the LORD" (1 Samuel 2:12). These two sons used their position as priests serving under their father to feed their gluttony and sexual lust. They disobeyed the law as to how the meat was to be eaten and they committed fornication at the entrance of the Tent of the Meeting with the women who worked there.

What occurs in 1 Samuel chapters 1-4 is a devasting unfolding of judgment upon an entire family line. Eli's two sons die under God's judgment, as does overweight Eli himself who dies violently by falling backwards and breaking his neck upon hearing of the death of his sons. His heritage is cursed with the promise that they will suffer these premature deaths. The story of Eli and his sons reveals that Eli's own lack of modeling restricted him from restraining his sons in the areas of gluttony and sexual sin. He had lost credibility to speak to them. The recorded fact that he was extremely overweight in his old age likely meant that he also had a problem with gluttony. It appears to be a sad classic case of "like father, like sons." As for their loose behavior, the fact that Eli did not stop his sons after learning of what they were doing makes one wonder about what was going on with him sexually.

You can become like Eli if you know the truth and yet do not live it before your children.

Thankfully, the Bible also gives positive examples of father models. They are one biological father and two spiritual fathers.

The Father Modeling Hall of Fame

Abraham was the man whom God chose to be the father of all who believe. He chose him to be a faithful model and teacher to his child Isaac (Genesis 18:18-19) knowing that this simple father-to-son faithfulness was the key to the fathering of many nations of faith. The determining event in Abraham's life was when he was called to sacrifice his son Isaac on the mountain. God intervened and provided a ram to sacrifice instead. This made a profound impact upon his son Isaac. What his father modeled was absolute faithfulness to God no matter what. This was a lesson that Isaac never forgot. Abraham wasn't perfect but he was a positive model of full devotion to Another Father for his son Isaac.

The Lord Jesus Christ called His disciples "to be with Him" (Mark 3:14) so that they could simply listen to Him and watch Him model what He wanted to teach them. Though He ministered to crowds, He focused his modeling to these twelve men, and from among those men He chose three, Peter, James, and John. He devoted Himself to modeling the special things He wanted them to pass on to the next generation.

Jesus never asked His followers to do anything that He Himself had not showed them how to do first. He appeared to be a man almost consumed with the idea of modeling all that He taught to His disciples. He was simply doing what He saw the heavenly Father do for Him. "I tell you the truth, the Son can do nothing Himself, He can do only what He sees His Father doing, because whatever the Father does the Son also does" (1 John 5:19 NIV).

We do not know exactly how this worked. This is in the realm of mystery. We do know that the Father and the Son preexisted eternally together and this passage indicates that the Son follows the Father's modeling. Like Father, like Son. We also know that in Jesus' earthly life He, the Eternal Son, followed His Father's lead in all that He did. One such example is when He was being pressured by many to stay in the area where He was, but Jesus clearly followed Another Father's voice and left to go to other towns (Luke 4:42-44).

The Lord did not just tell His followers to love each other. He took the time on the very evening before His death on the cross to demonstrate to them what it looked like to love one another. He washed the feet of all the disciples including those of Judas Iscariot, his already arranged betrayer. "I have set you an example (model) that you should do as I have done for you" (John 13:17 NIV).

The Apostle Paul shows that he also understood the power of modeling. The Corinthian church was faced with a problem trying to decide whether a Christ-follower should eat meat that had already been sacrificed to idols. At the end of his argument, as he writes to help them work through such issues of conscience, Paul simply says, "Follow my example (model), as I follow the example of Christ" (1 Corinthians 11:1 NIV). Again, he modeled and taught the "like father, like son" principle.

Paul, the spiritual father of the Corinthian church, writes to them and says something fascinating relating to fathering and modeling. "Even though you have ten thousand guardians in Christ, you do not have many fathers. For in Christ Jesus I became your father through the gospel. Therefore I urge you to imitate me" (1 Corinthians 4:15-16 NIV). And then he proceeds to illustrate how this works out in his spiritual father-son relationship with Timothy. "For this reason I am sending to you Timothy, my son whom I love, who is faithful in the Lord. He will remind you of my way of life in Christ Jesus, which agrees with what I teach everywhere in every church" (1 Corinthians 4:17 NIV).

In every case in Scripture where the principle of modeling was followed there was a *multigenerational* impact of the ministry. Abraham's faithful fathering of Isaac reaches down to us today. He laid the foundation of the nation of Israel as the foundation for all Gentiles who would ever believe (Romans 4:11-12). The Lord Jesus' ministry extended beyond his thirty-three years of earthly life, including three years of public ministry, primarily because of the twelve men he called to be with Him as His first spiritual children reaching to us today. And the Apostle Paul's ministry impact did not end at his martyrdom but continued through his spiritual sons, Timothy, Titus, Silas and others before whom he modeled the life of Christ, impacting us still today.

Jesus told His disciples, "…Unless a kernel of wheat falls to the ground and dies, it remains only as single seed, but if it dies, it produces many seeds" (John 12:24). Jesus was talking about men's lives, not wheat. If you choose to do what you want to do (your own self-centered goals and desires), selfishly ignoring what you are modeling to your children, you remain intact and yet you remain "a single seed." There is no life perpetuated. You will have no lasting positive multigenerational influence when it comes to your family, no matter what you accomplish or achieve in other realms.

The Rewards Of Modeling Integrity To Our Children

The first reward as we have just mentioned is the satisfaction of your life having a multigenerational impact upon your children, grandchildren, and beyond.

A second reward for positive modeling is that the man who chooses to model godliness to his children enters into a mysterious identification with the heavenly Father. His knowledge of the heavenly Father changes from intellectual understanding to a living relationship. Do you know how it is when you come to a realization of something that you thought you already knew? But once you actually have a particular experience, now you know it?

There was a time a number of years ago when I was just out of college and in business with my father. I was struggling with some issues relating to the business venture we were doing together and I needed his counsel. The only problem was that he was consumed by the needs of the company that he had founded which was undergoing a major crisis. He had been retired for ten years, and was living in Hawaii but he still sat on the board of directors of Sambo's Restaurants. Even though I had some empathy for what he was going through, I was so caught up in my own needs I could not begin to understand what he must be going through seeing something that he had built being destroyed right under his nose. He was not being listened to. He was looked on as an outsider by the company he had help build, in which he had invested so much of himself. (The name "Bo" in the name came from his last name.) The result was that Sambo's Restaurants, Inc. began its six-year slide into ultimate bankruptcy.

Some twenty plus years later I found myself in a parallel, though quite different situation. As the only remaining elder of a church that had lost the founding pastor and the other elders under less than ideal circumstances, I found myself struggling against criticism that seemed to come at me from every side. In the middle of it all, I can remember talking on my cell phone while I was picking up my children from school. They needed me but I was caught up in my other world. It was then that I connected to the feelings my dad must have felt back then and it was as if I had just stepped into his shoes.

I now *really* knew my dad through a shared similar experience. What my father had experienced was no longer head knowledge for me. It had finally reached my heart twenty years later! That is what choosing to model to your children is like. You enter into the heavenly Father's experience of modeling to His Son. From eternity past until now He models to His Son (John 5:19). This is a mystery but it is true. When you model to your children then you unite with the Father's heart through shared experience. You are just being like your dad. Like Father, like son.

A third reward is to have a built-in motivation to live a holy life. The Lord Jesus prayed to the Father the night before He went to the cross, the night before He paved the way for our salvation, saying, "For them I sanctify Myself that they too may be truly sanctified" (John 17:19 NIV). He then prayed not just for His spiritual children but for His spiritual grandchildren, great-grandchildren and beyond (John 17:20).

The reward is that when we choose to model godliness, we sanctify ourselves, that is, we set ourselves apart for an intimate relationship with God. But that does not mean that our children will automatically follow because they have free will. But we will have greatly decreased the difficulty that they will have in reaching out to and following the Savior. A father who consciously models positively to his children will be continuously motivated to walk close to God, not only for his own sake but for theirs.

The fourth reward of modeling to your children is that you will tend to produce children with the motivation to live a life pleasing to God. If there ever was an example of a people who were discouraged because of their fathers who did not model, it was the religious leaders, spiritual fathers of Jesus' day. Jesus said it like this: "The teachers of the law and the Pharisees sit in Moses' seat so you must obey them and do everything they tell you. But do not do what they do for they do not practice what they preach. They tie up heavy loads and put them on men's shoulders, but they themselves are not willing to lift a finger to move them" (Matthew 23:2-4 NIV). Jesus proclaimed the "like father, like son" principle when he told the Pharisees that their zeal to make converts was only going to produce spiritual children who were "twice the sons of hell as they are" (Matthew 23:15 NIV).

When I talk to a group of men and ask this question, "How many can remember your father ever coming to you and asking for forgiveness?" It is amazing to me that hands rarely ever go up. This to me is very sad. How different you might be to your children if you moved into the light (exposure of our sin by God's Word) and humbly confessed it and turned from it in front of your children. Think of the following Bible passage as a father relating to his children: "If we claim to have fellowship with God yet walk in darkness, we lie and do not live by the truth.

But, if we walk in the light, as He is in the light we have fellowship with one another and the blood of Jesus, His Son, purifies us from all sin" (1 John 1:6-7 NIV).

WALK A LITTLE PLAINER DADDY

Anonymous

"Walk a little plainer, Daddy,"
Said a little boy so frail.
"I'm following in your footsteps
And I don't want to fail.
Sometimes your steps are very plain;
Sometimes they are hard to see;
So walk a little plainer, Daddy,
For you are leading me.
I know that once you walked this way many years ago,
And what you did along the way
I'd really like to know:
For sometimes when I am tempted
I don't know what to do
So walk a little plainer, Daddy,
For I must follow you.
Someday when I'm grown up
You are like I want to be.
Then I will have a little boy
Who will want to follow me
And I would want to lead him right
And help him to be true.
So walk a little plainer, Daddy
For We must follow you."

A Father's Prayer of Transformation

Dear Father,

I Praise You that in a world that is under the temporary control of a lying deceiver, I can fully rely upon You to be faithful and true. (Number 23:19, Titus 1:2). I praise You that when everything is shifting and changing You are the one constant who can always be counted upon (James 1:17).

I praise You, Lord, that You didn't just tell us the way to go but You showed us and became the way out of our sin and hopeless separation from You (John 14:6). I praise You that You chose to become one of us. You didn't do this for the angels but amazingly in your infinite mercy You did this for us (John 1:14). You aren't even ashamed to call us Your brothers. (Hebrews 2:11). By humbling Yourself for us in this way and going to the cross and taking our place You have gone before us to glory and are now preparing a place for us (Philippians 2:5-11, John 14:3).

I praise You, Father, that I can confidently follow the footsteps of Your Son, Jesus (1 Peter 2:21, 1 John 2:6), that You have shown me through Your Word with directions that are made clear as I listen to the guidance of Your Holy Spirit (1 John 2:26-29).

But, dear Father, I confess that I have lowered my sights and chosen at times to follow lesser models, media figures, cultural norms and, of course, my own father. I realize that if I follow these models as my guide I will cause my children to stumble. I have selfishly forgotten the importance of what I model to them and have neglected to be the model that they need me to be. Instead I have often been a stumbling block to their simple faith in You (Matthew 18:1-14).

Oh Lord, help me to turn from living for myself to living for You, to seeing my life set apart unto You so that I can be a model for my children and grandchildren to follow (John 17:19). I want to do this not just for them but for the lives they will touch (John 17:20). Father, I can do this only through the life and power of Your Son living in and through me (Galatians 2:20, John 15:5).

In Your Son's Holy Name, Amen.

EQUIPPING SPIRITUALLY

"Fathers do not exasperate your children; instead bring them up in the training and instruction of the Lord"

(Ephesians 6:4 NIV)

Stepping Stone or Slippery Rock?

Imagine a narrow, fast-flowing stream. In the middle of the rushing white water is a solid, flat rock placed right at the midpoint between the two banks, just the right distance for a person to put his foot on and then from there step safely on to the other bank. The stream must be crossed and the other bank represents ultimate safety. A father can be like that stepping-stone, perfectly set in the middle of the stream that his children can confidently step out on and spring forward into eternal fellowship with the heavenly Father through His Son.

Now picture yourself standing on the bank of that same narrow stream but this time there is a different rock in the middle of the flow. This one is jagged, sharp, wet, and hard to get a foot on. Rather than being a safe transition to the other side, it is a rock that will cause a person to slip, fall, and be caught up in the raging stream and possibly drown. It is a slippery rock that causes hurt and projects danger rather than safety.

A religious father who is not faithfully portraying the heavenly Father's heart to his children is in real danger of being that slippery rock. His children will assume that he is an accurate portrayal of the Father God rather than an inaccurate betrayal of the heavenly Father's character. They will tend to believe more in what they see rather than what they cannot see. Conversely, an irreligious father makes no pretense of portraying the heavenly Father to his family. He can definitely be a slippery rock as well, but not to the extent that a religious father can be. This had to be one of the reasons the Lord Jesus was particularly tough on the religious Jews during his years of ministry. For sure the Lord hates slippery rocks (see Matthew 18:1-14).

These two rocks represent the two spiritual directions a father can take his children, to life or to death. He can help their journey of faith or hinder it. A father's influence is never neutral. Fathers have tremendous influence upon the spiritual destinies of their children.

However, increasingly the role of the father as a spiritual shaper of his children is undergoing a challenge. Judith Rich Harris, in her book entitled *The Nurture Assumption: Why Children Turn Out The Way They Do And Parents Matter Less Than You Think And Peers Matter More*, (The Free Press, 1998), says that parents have given way to peers as the primary molders of children in the 21st century. Ms. Harris makes a legitimate case. She uses some carefully selected and edited studies to buttress her thesis that it is peers rather than parents who are shaping children today.

Making A Spiritual Difference

Maybe Ms. Harris has a point. Peers are indeed having an influence upon our children. Maybe the forces that are working against us are just too powerful to fight. Although she did not use biblical examples to back up her arguments, I can help her out with some biblical support for her thesis. One could make a case from the Bible that fathers do not make that big a difference in determining the spiritual future of their children.

Ungodly fathers who had godly sons-
    Amon (ungodly father), Josiah (godly son) (2 Kings 20-22)
    Ahaz (ungodly father), Hezekiah (godly son (2 Kings 16:2,4)
    Abijah (ungodly father), Asa (godly son) (1 Kings 15)
    Saul (ungodly father), Jonathan (godly son) (1 Samuel 15-19)

Godly fathers who had ungodly sons-
    Isaac (godly father), Esau (ungodly son) (Genesis 25)
    Samuel (godly father), Joel and Abijah (ungodly sons) (1 Samuel 8:1-5)
    David (godly father), Absalom (ungodly son) (2 Samuel 18, 1 Kings 1)
    Hezekiah (godly father), Manasseh (ungodly son) (2 Kings 21:2-5)

Before we look at the case for the priceless value of a father taking responsibility for his children's spiritual development it is important to understand that the Scriptures present a paradox when it comes to the parental spiritual impact upon children. They teach two things that on the surface appear to be contradictory but in reality are complementary.

The Bible teaches that a father's sinful choices will impact his family to the fourth generation (Exodus 34:7). And Scripture teaches that a father's righteous life will bless his family to the fourth generation (Psalm 78:5-6).

But there is another truth to consider. A father's choice is still his choice and not his children's choice. Each individual is held accountable before God for his or her response to Him. The scriptural support for this is overwhelming (Ezekiel 18:20, Genesis 4:7; Ephesians 6:1,4; Romans 14:12; 1 Corinthians 4:5, 2 Corinthians 5:10).

To hold the first truth without acknowledging the second would deny individual responsibility. To hold the second truth without accepting the first would deny family influence and solidarity. There are numerous examples in Scripture that give fathers hope that they really do make a difference to their children: Here are a few:

Abraham and his son Isaac and grandson Jacob (Genesis 22)
Noah and his three sons (Genesis 6, Hebrews 11:7)
Joshua and his family (Joshua 24:15)
Obed-Edom and his household (2 Samuel 6:11)
The Philippian jailer and his family (Acts 16;31, 34)
Crispus and his household (Acts 18:8)

Whole families are blessed, are spiritually impacted in a positive way, when a father turns to the Lord. This of course does not deny the freedom that each individual family member still retains to choose to follow or not to follow his God.

The fact is that if children are given a godly model by their father they will more easily learn love and truth in their lives than if they are not given that model. In his book, *Faith Of The Fatherless*, psychologist Dr. Paul Vitz says that he initially set out to examine the lives of prominent atheists of the last four centuries. The fascinating thing that he discovered was that these "evangelists of atheism"—Darwin, Huxley, Neitzche, and Freud—each had fathers who were either weak, abusive, missing, or dead. He then wondered if this finding was simply the normal condition of the time. What he found was that in contrast to the atheists, every one of the prominent theists of this period had strong, tender bonds with their fathers.

For example, Blaise Pascal, the French philosopher, mathematician, and defender of Christianity, was homeschooled by his Catholic father. C.K. Chesterton, the persuasive Christian apologist, was deeply attached to his father. Dietrich Bonhoeffer, the highly influential German theologian who was executed by Hitler, also came from a loving home. Vitz also gave several other examples.

The bottom line in his study is that men who grew up to be passionate atheists had either nonexistent or very poor relationships with their fathers, while men who grew up to courageously defend the Christian faith had had loving relationships with their fathers. Earthly bitterness produced heavenly blindness and earthly love gave heavenly light.

In another book, *Raising Faithful Kids In A Fast-Paced World*, the author, Dr. Paul Faulkner, pointed to a study on church attendance that compares a father's and a mother's spiritual influence upon the next generation as it relates to church attendance. According to this study, if both the mother and father go to church, seventy-two percent of the children will go when they are grown. If only the father goes, that percentage does not drop too much, as fifty-five percent of the children will go to church. But, amazingly, if only the mother attends church, only fifteen percent of those children will be churchgoers when they are grown. Like father, like son and daughter.

Think about how your father's faith has affected your journey. I can almost guarantee that if your father did not show a commitment to attend church, you struggle with consistency in that area. Young men naturally want to emulate their fathers. If a father's faith is not real in a way that reflects a commitment to weekly worship then he becomes a slippery rock rather than a stepping-stone to his children living as godly adults.

Though my father would readily admit that it was my mother who possessed the more evangelistic faith of the two, I appreciate him for the value he placed upon attendance at weekly worship as a family during my youth. He put me in a place, often against my will for many years, to be able to hear the word of God and eventually respond with faith of my own.

A 1988 study by Cynthia Clark shows that my experience is not unique when it comes to my father's greatest spiritual influence being attendance at church that was both modeled and mandatory.[1] This is a good news/bad news kind of study that shows that fathers do make a significant contribution in this area of public worship. However, it also reveals that fathers today have a tendency to over-delegate deep spiritual equipping more to the "professionals" (pastors, children's and youth workers).

So clearly fathers do make a significant difference in the spiritual life of a child, and yet there appears to be a large gap between the potential impact they could make and the actual spiritual influence they are having.

Children's Spiritual Need for a Father

Children desperately need their fathers for their eternal good. Yes, God can and does bypass a negligent father and use others in the lives of His dear children to bring about His purposes in their lives. I have seen firsthand how He works around abusive and absent fathers and through other means reveals His Father love. But this is not the ideal design and a father who fails in his responsibility should never presume on the grace of God that his children will know God through other means.

The Bible states that when fathers' hearts were not turned to their children the land of Israel would be cursed with broken families (Malachi 4:6) and the hearts of people would be unprepared for the Lord (Luke 1:17). When we look at these prophecies, four hundred years apart, one referring to Elijah and the other to John the Baptist who ministered "in the power of Elijah," we are able to see the strategic role fathers are to play in their children's spiritual lives.

The Scriptures give us a picture of what families look like where fathers have abandoned their spiritual posts. First of all, fathers in Malachi's day did not see their own sinfulness and their desperate need for the grace and mercy of another Father. The Israelites had become complacent in their attitude toward sin. They did not take the sacrifices seriously as they brought crippled and diseased animals for the priests to sacrifice (Malachi 1:8). They looked at worship of a holy God as an unreasonable burden. These fathers were like the people Agur describes as "pure in their own eyes and yet not cleansed of their filth" (Proverbs 30:12 NIV).

A father whose heart is turned to his children will carry with him a sense of personal responsibility for his sin and will communicate to his children that sin is nothing to be trifled with. Children know that their fathers sin. If a father treats his sin lightly or with an attitude of self-justification, then that is the same attitude toward sin his children will learn. Like father, like son and daughter. And when sin is viewed in this way, the provision of the sacrifice of Christ is not good news. It is an offer from God that seems unnecessary, superfluous and irrelevant.

Dad, you need to be accountable to your wife and your children. When (notice I didn't say "if"!) you wrongly offend them you need to have the courage to go to them and ask for forgiveness. This models to them what they need to do when they sin against you or others. An encouragement: If you have asked forgiveness of your wife or children recently you are modeling strength, not weakness. You are being a real man!

Second, Malachi described what family breakdown looks like. Divorce was rampant in Israel in his day, with men divorcing their wives over petty issues, ignoring God's command against divorce. It appears that these men were looking for an easy out, perhaps wanting to trade in their forty –year-old wives for more attractive twenty-year-old models. They found lifetime commitment to one woman to be restrictive and inconsistent with their pursuit of pleasure and personal fulfillment (Malachi 2:15-16). Doesn't this sound like 21st Century America?

A father is also able to provide his children with a picture of a life voluntarily and joyfully submitted to God's authority. This includes a lifetime commitment to one woman. But it takes two people to make this a reality. Tragically, sometimes this is not possible when a wife chooses to leave or becomes unfaithful by hardening her heart. The honoring of his parents and the faithful discipline of his children are also lifelong commitments a father must model.

When a father lives this kind of life of submission to God he is personally demonstrating to his children that the heavenly Father can be fully trusted as ruler over their lives. He communicates to his children that God is good and worthy of trust and obedience.

When a father willingly submits to the heavenly Father he is essentially saying to his children, "Come on in; the water's fine." He becomes like the apostle John who wrote in his letter, "We proclaim to you what we have seen and heard, so that you may have fellowship with us. And our fellowship is with the Father and with His Son, Jesus Christ" (1 John 1:3 NIV).

On the other hand, if a father models selfishness and self-rule instead of submission to God's authority, he is setting his children up to look at the Lordship of Jesus Christ as a threat to their own dominion of self-rule. The gospel to is not good news to a child who has grown up with this kind of father.

Malachi 2:16 (NIV) is often quoted by people who are standing against the scourge of divorce. But what is often left out is the second part of the verse: "'I hate divorce,' says the LORD God of Israel, 'AND I hate man's covering himself with violence as well as with a garment,' says the LORD God Almighty. So guard yourself in your spirit and do not break faith." God hates it when a husband abuses and controls his wife as much as when he divorces her.

Again, Agur described a person who curses his parents and is pure in his own eyes and is arrogant and proud like this: "Their teeth are swords and their jaws are set with knives to devour the poor from the earth, the needy from mankind" (Proverbs 30:14 NIV).

In these two passages men are seen using their strength to oppress, control, and abuse others. So what children really need from a father is to be able to experience his strength in a way that is humble, sacrificial, and loving. This is what Jesus showed to us when he gave Himself voluntarily on the cross to meet our greatest need, that of payment for our sin. He demonstrated that masculine strength could be submitted to a higher authority, to the heavenly Father, to accomplish a gracious and merciful end, dying on the cross for our salvation. For children to see for themselves this sacrificial love in their father prepares them to recognize Jesus, who came in sacrificial strength at the cross.

There are many children and adults who are not able to truly believe that an all powerful God, who could squish us like ants if He so chose, became one of us, taking the cruel punishment that we each deserved so that every one of us could live with Him forever.

In summary, fathers help their children understand the seriousness of sin, teach them about the blessing of living under God's authority, and show them the glory of sacrificial love. If a father's heart is not turned toward his children he will have a tendency to teach an indifference toward sin, an unwillingness to submit to God's authority, and he will model the use of his strength to control or abuse others. These are the very opposite of what God intended. Sadly, these fathers become dangerous slippery rocks in the lives of their children.

A Father's Spiritual Needs

Spiritual equipping is not a one-way street. In my story in the introduction, little did I realize that I desperately needed what my four-year-old daughter Heidi could teach me. It was her innocent, trusting dependence upon me that God used to draw me back from my cynicism and blame-filled sense of being a victim in my marriage. It is not what she said but it was who she was and the important place she put me in her little world that broke through my selfish pride. She communicated to me a trust that her daddy loved her and would not do anything to hurt her. At a time when I was disillusioned with my marriage and confused vocationally, she provided a perspective I desperately needed just by her being who she was and unknowingly reminding me of my high calling as her Daddy. In her world no excuses would do. I was her Daddy, and Daddies don't just leave.

In his book, *The Good Family Man*, author Dr. David Blankenhorn says that children endow a man's life with meaning larger than his own self. He believes that children give significance to the more mundane qualities of everyday life. They make it possible for a man to believe he has a life that is good and purposeful.

This mutual spiritual benefit, of fathers to children and children to fathers, is what King Solomon referred to in his proverb when he said, "Grandchildren are a crown to the aged and parents are the pride of their children" (Proverbs 17:6 NIV).

And the Lord Jesus Himself tells His disciples, and us, that we have much to learn from children. When teaching about humility, faith, and kingdom greatness, Jesus called a child to stand in the midst of the crowd and said, "Unless you change and become like little children, you cannot enter the kingdom of heaven. Therefore, whoever humbles himself like this child is the greatest in the kingdom of heaven" (Matthew 18:3-4 NIV).

The Lord even referred to His own spiritual fatherhood of His disciples as a motivation for Him to be set apart before His Father. Life was not just about Him and the Father, but as a Father Himself, He knew all that He did had an eternal impact upon His beloved children. "For them I sanctify Myself that they too may be truly sanctified. My prayer is not for them alone but for those who believe on me through their message" (John 17:19-20 NIV). In His full humanity He chose to "need" his disciples, his spiritual children. This is a mystery and yet nevertheless, true.

Dad, you need your kids. Your children lead you to know the heart of the heavenly Father to understand more fully your royal sonship. They are gifts from Him to help mold you to become all that you were created and redeemed to be. You should welcome their presence, their inconveniences (including times of discipline), their silliness, their laughter, their relentless questions and, yes, even their silence when they become teens. "Whoever welcomes one of these little ones in My name, welcomes Me (Jesus) and whoever welcomes Me, does not (only) welcome Me but the One (the Heavenly Father) who sent Me" (Mark 9:37 NIV, parenthetic statements added).

Practical Help

There are a number of practical ways that you can equip your children spiritually. I have read several books that give many lofty ideas and recommend things that regular dads will simply seldom do. That is not the intention here. My desire is to acquaint you with some basic principles that can be applied so that when you dare to follow them they will become transformational for your family.

Spiritual Principles To Follow

Make your own spiritual growth a number one priority—I call this "sanctified selfishness." You should not feel guilty for appropriate amounts of time spent at home in the Bible and prayer. This needs to take priority over everything else, and this pays the greatest dividends in your children's lives through what you model and from the overflow they receive from your time spent with God. Think of it like the airline safety instruction we receive when we get on a plane. We are told that the adult is to put his or her mask on first in order to be able to assist the child without passing out.

"These commandments that I give you today *are to be upon your hearts.* Impress them on your children. Talk about them when you sit at home and when you walk along the road, when you lie down and when you get up" (Deuteronomy 6:6-7 NIV emphasis added).

You cannot fool your children. They know what is really important in your life. They need to know that your number-one passion is your relationship with Another Father. The apostle Paul's challenge to Timothy can just as well be applied to fathers, "Watch your life and doctrine closely. Persevere in them, because if you do, *you will save both yourself and your hearers*" (1 Timothy 4:16 NIV emphasis added).

Unfortunately there are many fathers who think they have a relationship with God but who have never allowed what may be in their heads to travel the eighteen inches to their hearts. Do you not realize that Christ Jesus is in you, unless of course you fail the test" (2 Corinthians 13:5 NIV).

You may be reading this and you are unsure of your relationship with Jesus Christ. You understand the facts of the gospel but you are not sure that you have ever personally chosen Christ to be your own Savior and Lord. To respond to Him is as simple as ABC.

A. **Admit that you are a sinner** - According to Romans 3:23 you have sinned and fallen short of God's perfect standard of holiness. Only one sin makes you a sinner just as only one murder makes a person a murderer. According to Romans 6:23 your sin has earned you eternal separation from God, which the Bible calls "death."

B. **Believe that Jesus Christ is your Savior and Lord** - According to Romans 5:8, Jesus died for your sins. He was sent by the Father for that very purpose, to do for you what you could never do for yourself, making the way to be right with God. He is the only way to the Father (John 14:6).

C. **Call upon Christ to be your Savior and Lord** - It is not enough to believe intellectually this message any more than it is enough to believe that a plane will take you from one place to another. You need to put your full trust in the plane and put your weight onto one of its seats to make that belief effective in getting you to your destination! The gift of eternal life is received when you reach out in simple faith and ask Christ to save you, to forgive you of your sins, and to rule your life now through His resurrected power. "Everyone who calls on the name of the Lord will be saved" (Romans 10:13 NIV).

If this "ABC" Truth reflects the desire of your heart, to respond you may pray the following by reading these words to the Lord right now. There is nothing magical about the words. The important thing is the sincerity of your heart as you express your heart to the Lord.

Dear Lord Jesus,

I believe You are the one who has revealed the heavenly Father to the world and You are the only way to know the Father. You died on the cross and rose from the grave to bring me into relationship with God the Father, so that I could be forgiven of all of my sins and He could become my Father. I ask that You become my Lord and Savior and save me from the judgment I so justly deserve. Show me how to be the man You desire me to be and empower me to truly love my family and others as You would have me to do. In Your Holy Name, Amen.

He has promised that He will respond to your simple faith in Him and He does not lie. If you do this it is very important to let someone who is a follower of Christ know that you have received Jesus as your Savior and Lord. Men, we need each other as we walk this spiritual journey.

Pray with your wife – The power to equip your children spiritually is activated when a husband and wife pray together. Every marriage has different challenges in this area. I confess that I often fail to take the initiative. The obstacles are legion: fatigue, time pressure, guilt, marital conflict, habit, distractions, to name but a few. Yet the influence of a couple praying together for their children is greater than both of them praying individually. There is a special Niagara Falls-like power and presence of God in our families that is harnessed for the eternal good of our children when husbands and wives pray together.

In the Bible, Solomon said, "Two are better than one, because they have a good return for their work. Though one may be overpowered, two can defend themselves. A cord of three strands is not quickly broken" (Ecclesiastes 4:10,12 NIV). And Jesus tells us, "For where two or three come together in my name I am with them" (Matthew 18:20 NIV).

Pray with your children -This is something so simple to do and yet so neglected. When I would hold regular fathering forums, I asked men if they could recall a time when their fathers prayed with them. Again, the response was usually nil. This is tragic, and even churchgoing fathers fail to pray with their children.

I would then tell the men, "*You* can do something when you go home that your father never did with you and it will change the lives of your children. You can go to their bed, put your hand on them, and pray with them and for them." What a blessing it is for children to know that their father is going to Another Father on their behalf and showing them how to do the same. The opportunities are everywhere: in the morning before school, in the carpool, on the phone, at the dinner table and, of course, at bedtime.

For dads of young children, let me emphasize again the power of reading to them and then praying for them after you are done, before or after they fall off to sleep.

Guard the family meal times and use them to focus the family on God – If it is at all possible, have a regular family time where you make it a point to include some talk about spiritual things. To have just one time a week where you do this as a family would be more than ninety-five percent of believing families are doing. Your family will begin to look forward to it. There are many materials available for families to read together. At the Christian bookstore you can find some great devotional books appropriate to families or you may just want to share a Scripture that has been meaningful to you lately or one that you think applies to a current family issue.

Here are a few questions that you can ask your family that can be helpful. You could even ask a different question each night of the week at the dinner hour.

- *What are you thankful for tonight? Think back over the last week, what can you be grateful to God for? (1 Thessalonians 5:18)*
- *What are you worried about tonight? (Phil. 4:6-7)*
- *What is God teaching you? (Col. 3:16)*
- *What do we need to work on as a family? (Ephesians 6:4)*
- *Who do we know that we need to be praying for tonight? (Ephesians 6:18)*

As you share concerns use them as an opportunity to encourage and "catch family members doing something right" (Ephesians 4:15).

Take advantage of what the local church has to offer for your family - Cindy and I firmly believe in the vital importance of the local church when it comes to the spiritual growth of our family. We live in a time when there is much cynicism and criticism of the church. Part of the church's very purpose is to equip believers for ministry. Of course it is never to be a substitute for your role as parents (Ephesians 6:4) but it can be a wonderful complement. Dad, beware of the extreme of overdependence upon the church in equipping your children but also be aware of the opposite extreme of neglecting the church altogether. You will be modeling something very dangerous to your children if you do. You will be saying to them that they do not need the body of Christ for their spiritual growth and putting a slippery rock in their path. But the truth is that we do need the gifts and resources of a local church to partner with us.

In summary, spiritual leadership begins at home. This is the place it will be tested first. If a man cannot live lovingly lead his home he should not take his show on the road. That is clearly why when Paul outlines the responsibilities for spiritual leaders in the church. In 1 Timothy chapter 3 and Titus chapter 1, a man's marriage and family life are mentioned as key qualifications for spiritual leadership. I am afraid this is too often ignored in the church today at our own peril. Our world is waiting for homes who profess faith in God to become homes of genuine hope and love. And Dad you hold the key!

A Father's Prayer of Transformation

Dear Father,

I praise You that You are actively at work in molding and shaping me and my family to become like Your Son, Jesus (Romans 8:28-29). I believe that You are using every circumstance, encounter and experience to shape me and my children. I praise You that You are committed to bringing us to maturity as Your sons and daughters (Philippians 1:6). This is not some "have to" but a "want to" for us, as You have planted within our hearts as Your dear children the very desire to do what pleases You, Father (Philippians 2:13).

I praise You Father, that as I delight myself in You, You have promised to give me the desires of my heart, and my heart's desire is to please You by leading my family in their faith in You (Psalm 37:4).

But I confess, Father, that I often forget that You are the one at work in me to spiritually equip my children. I either neglect to point my children to You or I think it all depends upon me and I neglect to trust Your faithfulness to work in them. Teach me to bear the load of spiritual leadership of my family with Your dear Son, taking His yoke upon myself (Matthew 11:28-30).

I also confess that I have allowed my failings in this area in the past to be an excuse not to be faithful in the present and the future. For that I ask forgiveness and submit myself to You to enable me to be faithful in the remaining years of opportunity I have (Phil. 3:13-14).

And Father, teach me to celebrate the little steps, the small but significant steps of capturing the spiritual territory in my family (Deuteronomy 7:22), and let me not despise the day of small beginnings when I see progress in my children's lives (Zechariah 4:10). You know I only long to hear "well done" from You when my journey is over and I must give an account to You of how faithfully I led my family to know You (Matthew 25:21, 23 Romans 14:12).

In the wonderful name of my Lord and my Savior, Amen.

ABOUT THE AUTHOR

Jamie Bohnett is the director of the Bohnett Memorial Foundation and founder of The Fathering Forum. He has been married for 30 years to his wife, Cindy, is a father of four and grandfather of one. He has worked with men for the past 20 years in various small group settings and believes that fathers encouraging fathers to love their families and to follow "Another Father" offers the greatest hope today for genuine family transformation. He and his family live in Redmond, Washington.

About The Fathering Forum:

The Fathering Forum, founded by Jamie Bohnett of the Bohnett Memorial Foundation, has an interactive website (Fatheringforum.com) that provides an electronic newsletter to fathers, encouraging father-to-father communication on ways to build stronger family relationships. The Fathering Forum produces its own small group resources for fathers and provides downloadable audio teaching messages from various ministries for dads. All monies collected from book sales enable the Foundation to make additional grants to family-serving non-profit agencies. The Fathering Forum is also associated with the National Center For Fathering and helps promote the Center's small group materials for fathers.

The Fathering Forum's Convictions:

*Ordinary fathers of faith have extraordinary wisdom to share what can help all fathers, thereby pointing upwards to the source of that wisdom, the heavenly Father (Matthew 5:14-16)

*Fathers are best equipped to love their families simply by encouraging and praying for one another on a consistent basis (Hebrews 10:24-25)

*Any man will receive God's richest blessing upon his life when he dares to follow the pattern of Jesus Christ and chooses to sacrificially love and serve his family (Ephesians 5:1-2).

*Fathering provides a man a divinely designed opportunity to connect with the very heart of the heavenly Father (Mark 9:37).

*Fathering provides a man a God-ordained incentive to live a holy life (John 17:19-20).

Go to www. FatheringForum.com today and sign up for a free electronic newsletter or to order more father-equipping materials!

ENDNOTES

Chapter 1

1. Stevens, Paul, Married For Good Regent College Publishing, Vancouver BC, 1986, p. 65-66

Chapter 2

www.9-11commission.gov/report/911Report.pdf
1. archives.thedaily.washington.edu/2000/111400/N3.maritalsat.html
2. Macobby, Eleanor, The Two Sexes: Growing Apart, Coming Together, Harvard Press, Cambridge, MA 1999, p. 269
3. Gilligan, Carol L. In A Different Voice, Harvard Press, Cambridge, MA 1982

Chapter 5

1. Gossman, Fred Spoiled Rotten, Warner Books, New York, NY 1990, p. 105,107,112

Chapter 6

1. www.nces.ed.gov/pubs98/98701.pdf
2. www.cppp.org/kidscount/education/parental_involvement.html

Chapter 7

1. May, Steve The Story File, Hendrickson Publishing, Peabody, MA 2000

Chapter 8

1. www.fathers.com/articles/move.asp?cat=move=previous&artnum=50

Chapter 10

1. Smalley, Gary and Trent, John The Blessing, Nelson, Nashville, TN 1986, p. 42

Chapter 12

1. www.Fathers.com Canfield, Ken Fathers And Spiritual Equipping,

Copyright 2005 Pleasant Word
Written by Jamie Bohnett
The Bohnett Memorial Foundation/
Fathering Forum
7981 168th Ave. NE Suite 220
Redmond, WA 98052
Ph. 425-883-0208/Fax 425-883-2729
"http://www.fatheringforum.com"

To order additional copies of

LIKE FATHER, LIKE SON

Have your credit card ready and call:

1-877-421-READ (7323)

or please visit our web site at
www.pleasantword.com

Also available at:
www.amazon.com
and
www.barnesandnoble.com

Printed in the United States
52306LVS00004B/241-300

9 781414 104034